Marsh Tales

MARSH TALES

Market Hunting, Duck Trapping, and Gunning

BY

WILLIAM N. SMITH

With drawings by C. D. Clarke

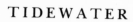

TIDEWATER PUBLISHERS

Centreville, Maryland

Library of Congress Cataloging in Publication Data

Smith, William N., 1951-
    Marsh tales.

    1. Market hunting (Game hunting)—Eastern Shore (Md. and Va.)—History.   2. Waterfowl shooting—Eastern Shore (Md. and Va.)—History.   3. Market hunting (Game hunting)—New York (State)—Long Island—History. 4. Waterfowl shooting—New York (State)—Long Island—History.   I. Title.
SK87.S65 1985   799'.09752'1   85-40531
ISBN 0-87033-338-0

Manufactured in the United States of America
First edition

For Becky

Contents

Locations of the Stories

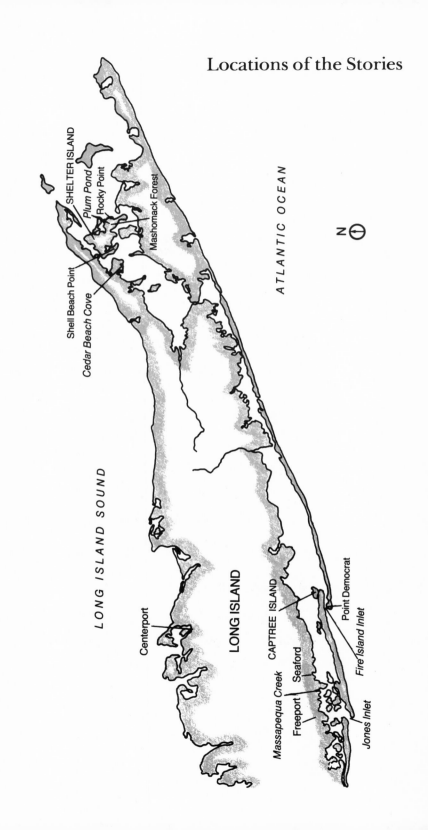

ATLANTIC OCEAN

N

LONG ISLAND SOUND

LONG ISLAND

SHELTER ISLAND
Plum Pond
Rocky Point
Mashomack Forest

Shell Beach Point
Cedar Beach Cove

Centerport

CAPTREE ISLAND

Massapequa Creek
Seaford
Freeport

Point Democrat
Fire Island Inlet
Jones Inlet

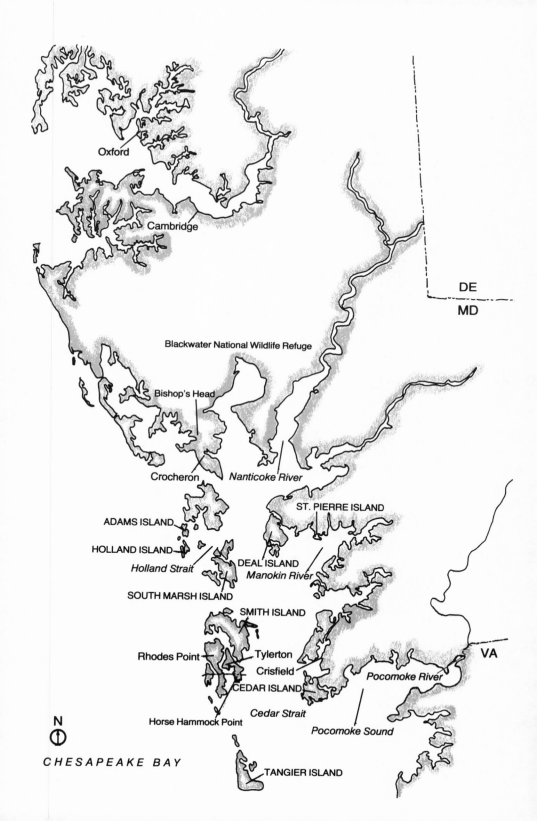

Oxford

Cambridge

DE
MD

Blackwater National Wildlife Refuge

Bishop's Head

Crocheron   *Nanticoke River*

ST. PIERRE ISLAND

ADAMS ISLAND

HOLLAND ISLAND

Holland Strait   DEAL ISLAND
                     Manokin River

SOUTH MARSH ISLAND

SMITH ISLAND

Rhodes Point   Tylerton

                Crisfield   *Pocomoke River*

CEDAR ISLAND   VA

                Cedar Strait

Horse Hammock Point

                                   Pocomoke Sound

N

CHESAPEAKE BAY

TANGIER ISLAND

Acknowledgment

THIS book would never have been possible without the help and dedication of many fine people. In addition to the storytellers who gave much of their time and themselves, and with whom I enormously enjoyed spending time and learning from, I'd like to thank each of the following for making an important contribution: Thomas Flowers; Bill and Judy Landon; Bill Merideth; George Combs, Jr.; Billy Richardson; Gib Clark; Jimmy Lankford and his family; Alan Smith; the boys in Cigar's shop; John Maddox of the Refuge Waterfowl Museum; Norman Moore; Courtney Hoblock; Marianne Czernin, my typist; Dick Tiernan; Chris and Iris Clark for the many nights of room and board, but especially Chris's devotion to this project which shows in his artwork; and, finally, and most important, my wife Becky for helping me to believe that this and many more books are possible.

Marsh Tales

Introduction

In *Marsh Tales* I have attempted to bring the reader into the world of the market hunter, duck trapper, and wildfowler of years past—the legal and illegal world of liberal shooting limits, or no limits at all, including shooting over baited waters—marshes, creeks, and rivers that were spotted yellow with corn. It was the world of unplugged shotguns, sink boxes—which were extremely effective devices—punt guns, battery guns, and shooting at night with gunning lamps.

The reader should keep in mind that until the late 1930s the commercial harvesting of waterfowl was a respected occupation throughout many of the rural waterfront communities from New England to the Carolinas. It was a pursuit that fed not only the patrons of gourmet restaurants and residents of foreign embassies, but also many local people as well, most of whom depended on the wildfowl as a mainstay of their diet. It was a way of life that was brought about mainly by the lack of economic alternatives in the communities, and by what seemed like an endless supply of waterfowl. It was, pure and simple, an opportunity to make a better-than-average day's pay for those who were skilled at it.

Countless creeks and tributaries, and thousands upon thousands of acres of marshland, made the Eastern Shore of Maryland and Virginia a perfect stopping place for migrating waterfowl. There was a clean, healthy Bay, and the marsh areas were alive with an abundance of the plant and underwa-

3

ter life crucial to sustain the millions of waterfowl who wintered there. As the megalopolis grew and alternate sites became limited, the area became even more important for the birds who, after their sojourn, were much stronger and healthier for the return trip north, in the spring, to their breeding grounds.

The Eastern Shore area, with its abundance of waterfowl, its geographic location, and its relative isolation was as perfect for the market hunter as it was for the fowl. At that time the area was almost a world unto itself, accessible only by sporadic ferry service or roundabout back roads. With more than fifteen rivers that meander through farmland and marsh into the Chesapeake Bay, it has almost four thousand miles of shoreline. A person who knew the area could be as elusive as a fox.

The accounts that follow are the unexpurgated recollections of men in the Long Island area (where I live) and on Maryland's Eastern Shore (where I do a lot of hunting). The selection of places from which to gather stories, therefore, took care of itself, although I am certain that similar episodes have occurred along the New Jersey coastal marsh area and on down from Currituck to Jekyll Island—to say nothing of along the great flyways of the Middle West and the Gulf.

I make no apologies or excuses for what is described here, and none of my story tellers would condone it if I did. These were experiences most of them were glad to have had, and they bring back fond memories of days, people, birds, and dogs long gone. Although scorned by some who self-righteously looked upon these activities and the men who engaged in them as the underside of our society, this was a way of life that was an important part of our social history—a remnant of the frontier—where men were extremely self-reliant, independent, and proud. As you will see, they were also full of high jinks, mischief, and life itself.

I hope these stories bring the reader some amusement, but more importantly, I hope they bring understanding and respect for these rugged men.

4

Bucky Clark

Bucky Clark was born on July 29, 1918, in Centerport, New York. He lived there with his family until he was seven years old at which time his father, a captain and fisherman, accepted a job on Shelter Island. He worked as caretaker of the twenty-five-hundred-acre estate known as Sachems Neck or Mashomack Forest which belonged to the late financier, Otto Kahn.

Growing up on Shelter Island, Bucky trapped, fished, and hunted the woods and waters in this area until leaving for service in Europe during World War II. A veteran of many of the big European battles, Bucky was wounded and was taken to England and eventually to the United States to be hospitalized.

When he returned to Shelter Island, he took over as care-taker and manager of the then Mashomack Gun Club, run by a wealthy New York family. It was here, in the manor house, that he and his wife Buzz raised their family of seven children, passing on to them their vast knowledge of the surrounding woods and waters.

He still lives in Mashomack woods with Buzz and can be found fishing, clamming, crabbing, and occasionally ducking.

WHEN he was alive, Otto Kahn was supposed to be the richest man in the world. He bought Mashomack from the Nicolls family as a real estate investment not to be used as a shooting club at all, just to have it as a place for him and his family to come to and use. He hired my father in 1925 to be the caretaker of the place, paid him $150.00 a month, which was unheard of back then. Plus, he paid for all our gas, gave us a car to use, a house to live in, and all the ducks and game we wanted to shoot. 'Course, he didn't know about that part. We never took advantage of it, though. At the time we shot the place for meat and nothing else. We'd never waste the game.

Black duck shooting was my favorite, and the most I ever got was eleven with one shot. They was sitting in an air hole in the pond, a big bunch of them, and I waited till they was all bunched together. Then I let 'em have it. Killed eleven stone dead and would have had twelve, but one cripple got away from me. Most times, though, I'd stool them at dusk. I'd take a pair of stool down to the pond or creek that I was gonna shoot and put them out on the opposite side of the water from where I'd be sitting. Then usually when they came in, the black duck would land and swim away from the stool. And this way I'd have them swimming right towards me. You know, a black duck's got an eye that's out of this world and when he's surveying a place over like that he can see everything. So you've really got to know what you're doing to outsmart them.

8

ONE MORNING, years back, when I was running the Mashomack Club, I had a man and his son down at Rocky Point rigged out for black ducks. It was one of those perfect gunning days, grey sky, raw cold, wind howling out of the northwest at about forty knots. I started thinking about these two out there, and since I had nothing else to do that morning, I grabbed my gun and a load of shells and headed off to join them. As I walked up on them I could hear their double barrels going off almost nonstop. My heart started beating a little faster, and I hurried up to get down with them. But as I sat down between them, I couldn't believe my eyes. Those black ducks were coming in steady in two's, three's, four's, and five's. Just pouring into the stool, low over the water, too. Not even the shooting was scaring them. Christ, you'd think there was corn there for them, but I swear there wasn't.

Anyway, these two were the worst damn shots I'd ever seen. Shootin' almost five boxes of shells, they'd only killed two birds. Now, this was too good to pass up, so I made a deal with them that I'd let them empty their barrels first, then I'd shoot. They agreed, and, man, that was the beginning of some fine shooting. They'd shoot, miss, and I'd shoot and kill almost every bird. It was one of those days when I just couldn't miss. They were getting more and more pissed off at themselves for missing, but for me it was like shootin' chickens in a barnyard. I won't tell you how many we finally carried back to the manor house that morning, but we all made two trips.

9

I'VE worked with all kinds of thoroughbred dogs down at the club. Christ, we even had some Lab down there who was some kind of world champion. But, personally, I've always liked a mutt better for working. Fact is, it doesn't matter what type of dog you use really, 'cause that dog's only gonna know as much as you show him.

I had a mutt named Freckles once, who was the best damn retriever I ever saw. I've seen him go up against thoroughbred gun dogs on a pond and make them look silly retrieving ducks. All you had to do was take him down to a pond and tell him "ducks," and, boy, he could find 'em. He'd smell them out of places you'd never expect them to be.

One time down at Plum Pond I shot this black duck. Hit him in the wing so he could still travel pretty good. I saw him go down on the other side of the pond, so I sent Freckles after him. He got his scent and took off through the brush and cattails after him. Then I see him cut off and head up through the woods yippin' like crazy. "That son of a bitch," I said to myself. He jumped a squirrel or a mink and is off that duck. Boy, I was mad. I took after him cursing and yelling, but he just kept going. Sure enough, I come up to him, and now he's at this tree with a hole at the bottom of it, diggin' like mad. Dirt, branches, and acorns flying all over the place. He's yippin' and barking, pulling it apart with his teeth, making this hole bigger and bigger.

"You son of a bitch," I yelled at him.

But he didn't even turn around. I guess he was as mad at me as I was at him. I knew I was beat so I figured I'd help him out at least. So I went and got a limb, cut a split in the end of it with my knife, and put the limb up inside the tree. You can catch a squirrel a lot of times by doing this. You take that cut limb and start twistin' it inside the tree and that split will eventually catch that squirrel's hair and bind it up so you can pull him out.

Now, I've got this thing inside the tree and I'm twistin' and twistin'. When I pulled it down, damned if I didn't have a bunch of duck feathers! That duck had run through the woods and hidden right inside that tree, and Freckles knew it all the time. Well, I reached inside the tree now that I knew what was inside, and I pulled that duck out. And never again did I ever doubt that dog.

I WAS invited to a duck and pheasant shoot over in Connecticut once at a place owned by the man who invented and sold the erector sets—A. C. Gilbert. The man who invited me was named Helman Hardges. I used to guide for him quite a bit and enjoyed gunning with him. This place of Mr. Gilbert's was a big shooting preserve where they drove the pheasants and flighted the ducks. Mr. Hardges took his great big Chesapeake with him and I had my dog, Freckles. I'll never forget that day 'cause we shot 186 pheasants and 220 mallards. Quite a day's work! When it came time to leave, Mr. Gilbert gave us all the birds to take home, and we packed them in the back of Mr. Hardges's big Chrysler station wagon along with the two dogs. We thanked Mr. Gilbert over a couple of drinks for what had been a memorable day, and headed back towards New York and Shelter Island.

On the way back, we stopped in a small town for gas. The man who came out to pump the gas was an old local colored guy. He came up to the driver's side to ask me how much gas we wanted. But when he saw that big old Chesapeake inside, he backed right away fast.

"Is that dog all right?" he said. We assured him that he was and rolled down the back window so he could pet him. Then he went to pump the gas and that's when he saw the birds!

"Lord, man, where you all been hunting?" he asked. By this time I was feeling pretty good.

"What do you mean, where we been? Oh, those birds? Yeah, you know you guys really got a nice spot for bird hunting here. We came up a few hours ago from Long Island to try out this dog here and see if he could hunt. We found this spot down the road there that looked like it might have some birds in it, so we stopped, let the dogs out, and, I'll tell you, I think we had one of the best days hunting we've ever had."

"Man, you sure did!" he yelled. "Where was that spot? I'm gonna go right down there after work."

He was some excited. We laughed about that all the way home.

ONE real cold morning, Alfred Tuthill, Joe Avona, and me were down at Shell Beach Point shootin' whistlers. Alfred and I were shooting a double-barrel and Joe had his old Model 11. We were really cutting 'em down until Joe's Model 11 froze up. He tried thawing it out by puttin' it under his coat, holding it in his gloves, and blowing on it, but nothing would work. Finally, he came up with the idea that if he pissed on it, the warm piss would free it up. So, he laid her down and pissed all over it, and damned if it didn't free up. He was some proud of himself for doing it, too, until the next bird flew by. He raised up the gun, shot it, and piss went flying all over him!

Captain George W. Combs, Sr.

CAPTAIN GEORGE W. COMBS, SR. was born on March 10, 1911, in Freeport, Long Island, the eleventh generation of the Combs family to settle on the south shore since 1644.

Like his ancestors before him, Combs derived his livelihood primarily from the bays south of Freeport—fishing, boat building, decoy carving, and gunning. As a boy, he would load his skiff with food, guns, and shells on Friday afternoons, during the gunning seasons, and sail off to one of the shacks scattered along the bay to gun with one of the baymen till Sunday night, when he would return in time for school Monday morning.

He also helped his father Capt. Jack Combs operate rum-running boats for Bill McCoy. McCoy was the man reputed to have the best merchandise on "Rum Row," the famous rendezvous spot for buyers and sellers just outside the twelve-mile limit on Long Island's South Shore.

Today Captain George, as he is called, lives with Frances, his bride of fifty years, in his house on the Massapequa Creek where he enjoys the sounds and beauty of the bay as the seasons change. During warm weather he can still be found out on the water fishing, clamming, or crabbing, and in cool weather, in his shop carving or in the marsh gunning.

My grandfather, Captain George Combs I, was born in Freeport on May 4, 1848, in his grandfather's house. He spent his whole life on the bay north of Jones Inlet. Summers he'd jacklight blue claw crabs and eels to send into the New York City hotels. Then in early fall he'd start his market gunning mostly for plover and yellowlegs. They'd sail out in their cabin sloops and would gun usually from Point Democrat east to Fire Island Inlet. They'd stay usually two to three days and gun the whole time, sleep right on the boat decks in boxes filled with salt hay, and eat birds and salt port cooked in big metal pots. You see, snipe brought a pretty good price back then. They'd give you twenty-five cents a bird which was damn good money. And Christ, there were so many of them, especially the plover, that when they jumped off the bars, they would cover the sun. They'd sit out in the bay on the bars feeding until the tide would start to cover them. Then they'd jump up and fly into the marshes where the gunner'd be with all his stool set. They used muzzle guns, mostly ten, eleven, and twelve gauge. Shoot right into the flocks of them, then whistle 'em right back in and shoot 'em again. Christ, the yellowlegs would just keep coming back; the plover, they were a little harder. The most I think he ever shot in one day was one hundred and twenty-seven, which was pretty damn good.

Then, of course, they'd come home with the birds and the whole family would pitch in and help clean them. They'd sit around together picking and cleaning. 'Course, back then they had some pretty big families, you know.

Now, my grandfather owned a small icehouse in town, and he'd get all the local people to collect their condensed milk cans for him. And he'd put the birds in these with the feathers all around them to keep them dry and insulated. Then he'd store 'em in the icehouse till he was ready to take them to the market, which was usually on a Friday. He'd leave town at four A.M. on a stagecoach for the Washington Street Market in New York

City where he'd sell the birds to Knapp and Von Norstrand, who'd sell them to hotels, restaurants, foreign embassies, even the New York Athletic Club.

Now, during slow periods he'd carve his snipe, duck, and crane stool or shoot snowy egrets, seagulls, and starlings which he sold to W. W. Wilson and Company of Seaford. These would be sold as feathers for the Gibson Girl hat, and with this money he'd pay for his shot and powder.

WE SOLD black ducks during the Great Depression for one dollar a piece. 'Course back then a dollar looked almost as big as the Sunday funny paper. Canvasbacks, which are the biggest and finest eating ducks anywhere, would bring from a dollar fifty to two dollars depending on if they were cleaned or not. Cleaning wasn't generally a problem because there was usually a bunch of old-timers who would sit down at the water and pick and clean your birds for you just for the feathers. They used them for pillows, blankets, and mattresses, mostly the breast feathers. The others they'd throw away.

See, we gunned mostly black ducks 'cause then there was so many of them, and they brought such a good price. We had this one spot on the west side of what is now the Wantagh Bridge. It was a little island that has a fresh water vein that came up through it, and made a water hole, maybe two hundred feet long. It was the only fresh water hole out there that I knew of. Those black ducks would feed out in the bay on little clams all day, then come into this waterin' spot, and drink at night.

We'd walk the five miles out there at night in the most brutal weather you could imagine. Northwest wind blowing hard and raw cold with the bay frozen over. When you was out there, you shouldn't have been, that's for sure. We'd make up a little gunning spot to lie down in, in the grass, and wait for 'em. They'd fly in right over the tops of our heads, most times, and we'd start gunnin' the hell out of 'em, running back and forth, out onto the ice to pick up the birds, so they wouldn't scare the others off.

Our best night we killed fifty-five or sixty birds, but you had to work damn hard for 'em in that kind of weather. Yep, more than once I've come in from gunnin', taken a long serious look at my gun not knowing whether to throw it into the creek or not. But, next morning I was always back out there gunnin' something.

I REMEMBER it was 1932 or '33 because I had a '32 Chevy at the time, and it was just before I got married. It was one hell of a cold winter on Long Island that year with about fifteen inches of snow on the ground.

This one day I started out to go gunning. We were having a January thaw, real bluebird weather. So, I started off towards Freeport Point in my shirt sleeves where I kept my scoter decoys, but I brought plenty of other clothes with me in case it got cold again, you know. Well, I left pulling my scotter with me across the ice and walked down to Scallop Creek where I could see a couple of guys shooting whistlers. I walked up on 'em, and scared the hell out of 'em, before I saw that they were my uncle and cousin. So, talkin' to them after a little while, I left towards these other two guys I could see gunning. They spotted me coming and must have thought I was a game warden, 'cause they hid their bag of ducks and took off. They had a gunning boat with them mounted on a sled about three feet long and as they took off, stuff was falling all over the ice. I yelled to them finally, and they could have killed me for scaring them like that. But hell, I wasn't trying to at all. So anyway, they turned out to be friends of mine, Andy and Hogan. Now, by this time, it was getting damn cold, and we went back to the bank to get the bag of ducks. Well, Andy got wet getting them so I said let's go on up to that old gunning shack and get warm, which we did.

Well, every goddamn baymen's shack I've ever been in has an axe you couldn't cut yourself with if you had to. And, usually some sort of food like rice, flour, or salt pork and this was no exception. They usually had an old cook stove in 'em which should'a been in a dump. No firebricks, or rusting out, and always mounted on the south wall. So, if the wind blows out of the north the way it did that night, the heat goes right out of the place.

Well, we chopped up a load of wood, and shot a bunch of broadbill and brant out of an air hole off the dock and cooked 'em up for dinner that night. Had a hell of a good meal.

That night the wind started blowin' hard out of the northeast. So we put all the clothes we had with us on, made some blankets out of newspaper, and went to sleep. Now, Andy had a bald head, and the next morning when we woke up, I swear there was frost on it. It'd gotten so damn cold that night. Funniest damn thing you ever saw.

We got up that morning and walked across the channel to where there were quite a few summer houses that belonged to people we knew. We'd jimmy a door or window and go in and get something to eat or drink. Then, close the place back up. In this one place we found five bottles of gin, some crackers, and a whole mess of anchovy paste, so that night we had a pretty good time.

Next day we come up on this little house with three guys in it. They used it for washing oysters. Now, these guys were the type that could do pretty well with a bottle, and every time they got some money that's where it'd go. Well, we walked in on 'em, and they'd cut up every damn chair and table in the place for firewood, even with old rotted boats and shacks on the same island with 'em outside. All they had for a light was a coffee can with a little grease in it, and a rag stuck out of that. These guys were damn hungry. Anyway, we give 'em a load of ducks and stayed with 'em awhile, then headed back out to do some more gunning.

Now that night, Hogan and I was lying in the boat, with Andy in another one on the other end of the rig. Andy had this old single shot that he'd borrowed that kept jammin' up on him. He shot at this black duck and missed, and the gun jammed so I could see him trying to get the damn shell out with the plunger. Then, he loaded and shot at the other duck, missed him too, and they both finally jumped. I don't know what it is, but in real cold weather like that a black duck won't jump right away. Myself, I've shot one, reloaded, and shot the other right next to him. It's a funny thing, but I can remember my grandfather and father telling me the same thing. Maybe they don't hear the sound in real cold, foul weather like that.

After five days we went back to shore, and damned if we didn't find out people were real worried about us. My father told me later that he could see smoke coming from the shack from Freeport Point, and knew we were all right.

We had one hell of a time out there though, and I was only going to go for a half-day, you know.

WE KILLED a lot of brant and broadbill. You just wouldn't believe how many of them there was, and you could get seventy-five cents to a dollar a pair for them. We'd gun mostly out of a battery box* which was invented here in New York State in the early 1850s.

There wasn't any laws about using a battery east from Amityville and it was perfect for them cause the bay was wide open, not like up west where you have lots of little islands scattered around. You set the box out with a big rig of stool around it. And the eel grass, which was so damn long it floated right on the surface of the water, would break the waves down before they'd get to you. So you wouldn't swamp as easy as you might have otherwise. That grass would be covered with tiny snails and marine life, and that's what the birds loved to feed on. Whether it was floatin' in the bay or broken off and washed ashore they had plenty to eat from it. You could take your fingers and run them across it and pick off a dozen or more small snails. Not like the grass out there today. Now, it's short, and if it breaks off, it'll sink and rot on the bay bottom.

Back then the brant would be there in the spring too. Not like now when they come in the fall and winter. Christ, the only thing they've got to eat now out there is that damn sea cabbage which makes them as strong as an old-squaw. And if the bay freezes over, they'll come inland and feed off the sod farms. Which is okay, unless there's deep snow on 'em. Then they don't know enough to look someplace else. They'll just stay there and starve.

*A shooting box that sits flat in the water with a compartment for the hunter to sit or lie in so that his body is actually below the surface of the water.

ONE SUMMER, years ago, when I was a boy the weakfish just seemed to disappear from the bay. So, my Pop who had a big skiff, at the time, took us down to Beach Haven, New Jersey, south of Atlantic City, where he heard there were lots of fish. See, we sold shrimp in the summer for bait, and Pop heard they couldn't get any down there. So, off we went for what was suppose to be two weeks, but turned out to be eight or nine years of summers. When we first got down there Pop found us a big, old houseboat to live on until he later built us a house. Well, there were lots of fish down there, and we did pretty good selling shrimp to all the fishermen those summers.

There was one man, Brooks Van Noran, who came from an old well-to-do Dutch family from Catskill, New York, who fished his boat every summer out of Beach Haven and wintered down in Key West. He lived right on the boat, couldn't get him to sleep in a room for anything. Anyway, just after fishing, before he'd head for Florida, he always went home to do some gunning. And was always looking for somebody to go with him. So this one year I went up with him. Well, he always wanted to gun out of a battery but didn't have one so Pop came up and built him one, this same year.

I don't know if you've ever gunned that Hudson River, but they've got quite a variety of birds up there—redheads, pintails, you name it. They feed on the lily pads which are all over the place. One day we went out, set the box and our stool, and Brooks got in. And I took the boat ashore to watch and pick up birds. Now, every day the Hudson Day Liner would come by from Albany to New York, pulling a three-foot sea behind it. And when we saw it, whoever was on shore would run out and pick up the man in the battery. Well, this one day I didn't see it till it was too late. The boat came by, swamped the battery, which sunk along with two L.C. Smith ten gauges. Well, Brooks got out okay and luckily thought the whole thing as funny as I did.

BACK in the 1930s, we had a spell where the black ducks all but disappeared. You know, the government biologists say there's none around here now, but I've seen more lately than in the past five years. Well, during that spell we'd go down the bay and stay for a week sometimes and have a hell of a time just trying to get enough to live on.

Even the wardens knew it, and they wouldn't bother us, most of the time. Very few would bother you or try and set you up, although there were some that would. Hell, we'd even help them out, or pull them off some bar if they'd get stuck, cause they didn't have the best equipment. I always said, that just about the time a warden was gettin' smart about what was going on out there, that they'd either retire or die. 'Course, they weren't as bad as the damn cliff dwellers out there today.

As long as you didn't try and make fun of them they were pretty good. There might have been a lot of fighting with them, and I think two was even shot, but those weren't normal cases. What could really stir them up was the damn city people who'd come out on the trolleys and shoot every damn bird they'd see.

DURING Prohibition, my father Alvin, and I and some of his friends sailed down the bay on a fifty-eight-foot sloop to the Wa-Wa-Yonder Club north of Captree. The club was built in the early 1860s, by some members of the Southside Club, who wanted a place to do some bluefishing and weakfishing. They didn't use it much, maybe a little snipe shooting but that's about all.

Anyway, we'd go down there about once a year for a few days in the winter. Lay up and do some gunning. They had this caretaker down there named Lozy Raynor, who was a cousin of my Pop. Now old Lozy was quite a character and could put the liquor down pretty good too. Well, as we're tying up the sloop, old Lozy came walking down the dock, wanted to know if we had a drink. Back then, we always had plenty of liquor around 'cause my Pop was running rum. So we give him one, not too much though.

Now, there was also a warden who lived in the meadows around there named Johnny Shelf. We knew him pretty good 'cause he had pulled a couple of fast ones on my Pop. So we were careful about doing too much dusking, when he was around. He told us he was going ashore to town. And we asked him when he'd be coming back and to bring us a couple of pounds of butter. Not 'cause we needed it, we just wanted to know how long he'd be gone, you know. So, off he went for a couple of days, leaving us to keep an eye on everything.

That night we were sitting around playing poker about eleven o'clock when Mel said let's go up to Whirlpool Point and shoot us a bird. Now, during the day up there, you'd be hard pressed to see a bird, but at night they come in thick to a big air hole in the ice eating these mussels about one-half inch long, that lay in there by the thousands. So we headed off across the ice pulling my scotter and decoys. It was a real pretty night, clean and bright with a full moon. As we got up close to the point, we could hear the broadbill in there raising hell. Then, all of a sudden, they took off sounding like a damn freight car.

We set up our stool, some black duck and broadbill, and shot ourselves about ten black ducks in an hour and a half. Then all of a sudden, the broadbill started coming back. Fifty to one hundred fifty at a time, they'd land outside the stool and start fighting each other to get into the rig, splashing and jumping all over, really raising hell. To this day I've never seen anything like it. We killed seventy-odd birds that we knew of, till the wind turned northeast into our faces, and we couldn't see a damn thing. So, we picked up our birds and the rig, and headed back to the boat.

Well, just about as soon as we got back there that morning, Lozy came down asking for a drink. Mel had this horrible tastin' cough medicine with him and asked Lozy if he wanted a cordial. You see, we told him we was out of everything else. Lozy said what the hell, and Mel poured him a glass. He took a swig of it. His face turned all shapes, and he spit it out, shaking his head and yelling, "Goddamn it! I never did like that damn whore's drink anyway."

Do you believe in ESP? I'll tell you, I do. I knew this old man, named Scudder Miller, when I was real young. Old Scudder loved to gun, and he was a damn good shot. The slowest, most deliberate movin' man you ever saw, but a damn good shot. He had a heart attack one year, and the doctor told him, "Scudder, you'll never gun again." So Scudder sold his gunning boat and decoys, but kept his old L. C. Smith hammer gun. He was livin' down on the bay in his old houseboat and in not too much time he started to come back along pretty good. So, he bought himself some corn, threw it overboard and, Christ, he had some black ducks comin' around. He found an old sharpie [a type of boat], fixed it up, and I gave him about a half-dozen stool, and he killed himself some more ducks. Anyway, he also had this old cabin boat with an old 1924 Redwing motor in it and I guess it had been about three weeks since I'd seen him last and for some reason I headed down to his boat. Damned if I didn't find him face down in the boat, passed out. I picked him up and got him back into the houseboat, and he come out of it pretty good.

Then, about two years later, about five or six of us was out on my houseboat down the bay gunnin', and old Scudder was with us. We'd go down the bay for a few days at a time—gun, play cards, and drink a bit. Have ourselves a hell of a time.

This one night, Scudder and me went out together. It wasn't a bad night, but it was cold, wind blowin' about ten to twelve miles per hour and really pretty nice. Scudder set up on his spot, and I went down below him about a half a mile. I heard him shoot once or twice, and I shot a couple of times. Then, first thing I knew, for no reason at all, I heard him call out, "George."

Now, I could have hollered that, and there was no way he could've heard me, and I was a young man. We was just too far away from each other. Well, I grabbed up my stool and shoved up to him, and there he was, half overboard, arms dangling in the water. What had happened, I guess, was he'd gone to pick up a bird and had a heart attack. I brought him back to the houseboat fast as I could and gave him a little rye or something. Damned, if he didn't come out of it pretty good. Couple of days later, he was back gunnin' again. It was funny, though, how I could hear him cry out somehow, just as clear as day, 'cause he would've died right there if I hadn't found him.

Anyway, next year I had my houseboat down at North Creek. I had a few gunnin' parties and took them out from there. Well, I saw old Scudder one day. By now, he must have been seventy-five or seventy-six and I told him to stop down 'cause next day I only had one gunner, and we could go out together. He come down and stayed with me that day. We went out and got ourselves a bunch of oysters, and as we're sitting there, a pair of ducks came over us and landed in the marsh. Scudder says, "I'll go shoot them to have with the oysters."

He set off after them, snuck up on 'em, shot, and missed, which was something he rarely did. Well, he came back and, Jesus, was he upset. That just wasn't like him. Right after that, my gunner came down and that night we fried up the oysters with boiled potatoes for the three of us. After dinner, old Scudder said, "You know, that was the most food I've eaten in the past twenty years." You could tell he really enjoyed it. Next morning, we got up with the four o'clock alarm. Scudder got out of bed to light the old oil stove and, Christ, he passed out. I jumped out of bed, picked him up, but he was already dead. I put a mirror to his mouth and my ear to his heart, but, Christ, my heart was poundin' so loud I wouldn't have been able to hear him.

Well, this gunner that I had, Arthur Turner, was a wealthy man from the North Shore of the island. When he came to gun, he came on his boat dressed in Abercrombie & Fitch gunning clothes—took him two minutes just to take off his gloves. But he loved to gun. It was blowing damn hard, would've been a good morning for gunning, but I told him to take his boat home.

He took off and as soon as daylight came I headed over to the Coast Guard station to tell them what had happened. I told them, and the guy in charge says to me, "What the hell do you want me to do about it?"

Now, by this time I was damn mad 'cause I knew old Scudder was just layin' over in the boat, and I couldn't move him. Finally, this jerk got ahold of a trooper and he came over to my houseboat, lookin' everything over, and treatin' me like I killed the old guy. He wouldn't let me out of his sight for nothin', took me over to the troopers' barracks with him, and brought in the lieutenant who, when he saw me, said, "Jesus, I know you. You was runnin' rum here not too long ago."

They let me go after that and went back out and got old Scudder. But I always said that was ESP, 'cause each time he had the attacks I was there, and how else would I hear him call out?

LET ME tell you a story about George Pennall. He was a big man, stood about six feet, four inches tall and always perfectly dressed. He took a lot of wealthy people from the city and the island gunning, and was one hell of a shot himself. One of the great gunners from the Seaford-Massapequa area, and a good weakfisher, too.

He and a buddy of his took a load of minnows one winter and spread them over the meadows over Fort Neck. They waited till the first northwest wind blew, went down, and shot a farm wagon load of crows, over three hundred, and sold them for ten cents a piece to W. W. Wilson and Company, a hat company over in Seaford. They'd buy all types of birds for the feathers and stuff some of them and mount them right on the hats. That was a pretty big thing back then with the old-timers. My grandfather used to go out in the meadows, take a stick shaped like a T, put it into the ground, and wait for the starlings to land on it, like they do on the phone wire. Then they'd shoot the hell out of them. It was an easy way to make a little money then.

I'LL tell you another story about Arthur Turner, that wealthy gunner from the North Shore. The first year my wife and me was married, we lived down the bay on my houseboat. We'd gun every day down there, either with friends or takin' out huntin' parties. This one day, Arthur Turner come down with his wife. He was all dressed up as usual in his Abercrombie & Fitch clothes with his wife wearin' this beautiful full-length raccoon coat and carryin' the nicest little L.C. Smith twenty-gauge hammer gun I ever saw, all engraved. Real pretty. I took them out and dropped off her husband, and she stayed with me. Well, we're sitting there, and these three teal come in. I'm trying to point them out to her, but for some damn reason she couldn't see them. So, hell, I shot the three of them and told her to fire both barrels of her gun, which she did. Christ, her husband came back over, and when I told him she shot those three birds, he was happier than a pig in you know what.

Right after gunning, the bunch of us went and picked up a load of oysters to cook for dinner that night, along with this pile of crab meat that the Turners had brought down with them to make crab meat salad. Now, back in the boat we had two pails of water in the galley that we used for washin' up. One was clean and the other was slop water, stuff you'd already used. Anyway, I came in that night, washed the mud off my hands, and poured the dirty water into the slop pail. Now, as my wife and Mrs. Turner were makin' dinner, my wife noticed that as she was making the crab salad she'd take water out of the slop pail and put it into the crab meat. Meanwhile, she was trying to tip me off, but was afraid to offend the lady. So, later on, as we're eatin' oysters and crab meat, I'm sitting there eatin' away, not know what's happened and I can't for the life of me understand why my wife isn't eating the salad. Well, I'll tell you, to this day my wife still laughs like hell whenever that story comes up.

35

THERE was an old-timer around here who died around 1981, named Carl Chichester. He was the best damn blue-fisherman I've ever seen in my life. One tough son of a bitch and the meanest, most ornery person you'd every want to meet. He was fine as long as he made five dollars a day and you was makin' fifty cents, but if it was the other way around, he could be unbearable.

Anyway, one day me, Scudder Miller, the man who I told you about who had ESP, and Fred Karma were out gunning late in the fall when we came up on Carl and two or three other boats out on the bar settin' out soft clams. They'd use a motor mounted in the bottom of their sharpies and jet them right out of the sand, get twenty-five or thirty bushels a day sometimes. We pulled up alongside of them, and I yelled over to Carl to see if he'd seen any ducks around. "Oh, Jesus Christ," he says, "there ain't no goddamn birds around here anywhere. They been shootin' the hell out of this place at night and scared them all away."

I knew Carl pretty well, and about a half hour later I saw Ray Conrad around there and asked him the same thing. So he tells me, "George, every morning there's more goddamn ducks around here than you can imagine."

"Well," I told Scudder and Fred, "next morning instead of gettin' up at five, we'll get up around three-thirty or four and come down here." Which we did. Next morning we'd just set out, still dark and cold, and up come Carl. Holy Jesus, was he mad. He hadn't been gunning in six weeks 'cause he was makin' good money clammin'. Well, we killed a hell of a load of birds that mornin', and he didn't kill anything. Christ, he wouldn't talk to us for days. But he was some gunner.

I remember one day down at Cedar Beach Cove, he picked up about three hundred and seventy-five broadbill battery shootin'. Now that's just what he picked up, so you can imagine what he killed, and that's *one* man. He said the next day his head hurt so bad from shootin', he couldn't get out of bed. Some days he shot a case of shells easily.

WE was always pretty friendly with most of the wardens here. They were really a pretty good bunch of guys and real dedicated. They'd grab you if they could, but most of them would never try and set you up. I remember this one old guy, Charlie Weinburger, who was a real dedicated guy but not too smart, which made it good for us. Well, he grabbed me a couple of times for netting spearing illegally. You see, the law said you could use a net forty feet long for haulin' spearing, but nobody ever caught any amount with a net that size, so we'd always use nets one hundred feet long.

Now, the other problem that you had was the other bait catchers who was always a little jealous and would sometimes rat you out to the wardens, and that's what happened to me this one day. I had this old houseboat that I'd use for gunning and catching bait during the Great Depression, and if we made a little money, we considered ourselves real lucky. This one day, I was down past the Wantagh Bridge where I wasn't suppose to be in my garvey with my net. Well, I knew Charlie was around 'cause I could see him pretending he was fluke fishing with his deputy about three hundred yards away, and I heard his deputy say once over the outboard, "Let's grab him now." And this was before I even set.

See, I told you they wasn't too smart sometimes. Well, I got down past them where they couldn't see me, set the net, and hauled it, and Christ, I loaded up on that one haul. Put 'em in the bottom of my garvey and started back to my houseboat. Now, I don't see Charlie anymore, and I'm coming back through Deep Creek near Brant Point where I see some of the boys from Seaford and Freeport digging soft clams on the bar so I stopped to talk to them and told 'em to be careful 'cause I'd seen Charlie and the deputy, and I thought they was around somewhere. You see, most of the clams they was diggin' were between an inch and a half and an inch and three-quarters. Legal size was two inches.

Now, at the time I didn't know it, but Charlie and the deputy was layin' in a ditch nearby listenin' to this whole thing. See, he didn't see me after I moved to set my net so he was trying to get these guys for takin' undersize clams. Well, I took off again towards the houseboat in my rig which was a pretty fast little boat, and I see Charlie trying to catch me, waving his arms and yelling, "Stop, stop."

I told him, "Charlie, I can't stop now, I got spearing on, but if you want me, I'll be on the houseboat."

So, Jesus, down he come a little later with his deputy, and they tie up alongside the boat and come aboard. Trying to be real damn official.

He says to me, "George, I'm going to have to give you a ticket and confiscate your net."

Well, I told him he could give me the ticket if he had to, but there was no way he was takin' the net. And, with that, they jumped into the garvey to lift the net out, and I run over to their boat, untied the lines, getting ready to set it adrift. Christ, they jumped back out to get the boat, and as they did, I ran around the cabin, jumped into my boat, picked up the net, and threw it off on top of the cabin. Then I stood there and told them, "Damn it, if you want the —in' net, you'll have to wait till my pop gets here, and if he says it's okay, it's okay."

Now, remember, this is a damn state warden I'm talkin' to. So they didn't know what to do at this point, I guess, and they left with their tails between their legs. They were gone for about an hour and a half till my pop came. Then they showed up again, and Charlie says to my pop, "Captain Jack, I've got to give your boy a ticket."

Well, Pop says, "Goddamn it, if he did something wrong, give him the ticket, but did you see him doing something illegal?"

Finally, he admitted that he hadn't really, but he'd heard I was nettin' illegally, and he was pissed off 'cause he'd heard me

39

warning the other clammers. Well, that was the end of that and we all shook hands, and Charlie left again. Like I said, they wasn't bad guys.

Lennie Abbott

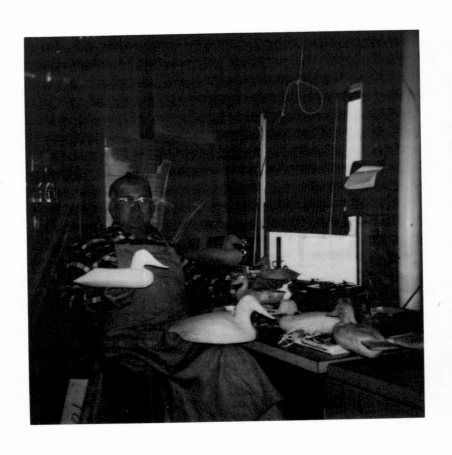

LENNIE ABBOTT was born in Oxford, Maryland, May 31, 1920. His family was originally from Deal Island, Maryland, home also of his gunner cousin, "Shimmey" Harrison.

A master of many trades, Abbott has been a boat builder, building over fifty boats when he owned an Oxford marina; shoe cobbler; electrician; welder; carpenter; waterman; and decoy carver. "When I come up, you had to do it all," he's fond of saying.

Today, he lives with Doris, his wife of 42 years, in Oxford, and stays busy crabbing, oystering, gunning, and carving decoys.

You KNOW, you hear all kinds of theories about what's killing the bay and making the grass disappear. Some say it's the farmers and their fertilizers running into the creeks, tributaries, and rivers. Others say it's the watermen with their pollution, or the shipping and its pollution, but I'll tell you what it is. The beginning of the end was that damn Chesapeake [and Delaware] Canal they cut through. It brings all the chemicals from Philadelphia, Wilmington, and that whole area. It's only common sense that all the crap has to come down through the canal and empty into the bay. And there's no way it cleans itself up before it empties into it either.

You know, there used to be wild rice growing all around the Susquehanna Flats. That was the main thing that kept all those canvasbacks up there. But now you'd be hard pressed to find any [rice] growing.

Another thing they screwed with that Canal is the tides. Before they built it, [the tides] moved around here no more than one knot. Now I'll bet it's over five knots, and what kind of effect do you think that's had on the bay?

I USED to make these decoys out of cork that I'd use over bait on the open water for black ducks and canvasbacks. They were twelve by twenty-four which is a damn big decoy. But, man, they could really pull the birds into that bait. I wouldn't paint 'em or nothing, but about three times a season I'd smoke 'em to keep that color into 'em and stop the water from sticking to 'em and freezing. I'd use two dozen for each set with twelve in each group and a hole for 'em to land in, in the middle. Those birds would come right into where I wanted them, especially those orange-leg Canadian black ducks. I'd sit there, sometimes with my dog, and we'd watch 'em dive for that bait. The water'd be about ten feet deep. Now, of course, a diver can just put its head down and roll under. They do it so naturally, but a black duck or a mallard ain't a diver. They're puddle ducks and feed in shallow water usually, but as long as you had corn for 'em to eat they'd do their damndest to go after it. It was really something to watch. See, they use their wings to push themselves under and each time they'd dive, there'd be a big splash of water—almost a bucketful. Under they'd go, and they'd get that corn. Don't think they wouldn't. It surprised me, too, at first, but they could dive ten feet or more if they had to.

I OWNED the old shipyard over there for years. I'd work hard in the boats all spring and summer, then as the weather started to run and fall was coming, I'd lay off the boats and start working on my decoys. Gettin' ready for gunning. We'd go shoot whistlers, blackheads, baldpates, geese, everything you can think of. Sometimes we'd bait 'em over corn, sometimes over tomato seeds. Oh, the birds love tomato seeds, and I'm not sure if there's a law against it or not still. See, when they had the tomato factories around here, skinning these tomatoes, they'd take the skin and the cores and get rid of 'em. The farmers would take 'em sometimes and use 'em as fertilizer in the fields or they'd dump 'em overboard and that's where we'd wait. Boy, you could put some hurting on 'em then.

OF ALL the gunning I'd liked the black duck shooting the best, and I'll tell you why. You could kill the black duck in warmer weather, and you could do it a lot easier. He's a big duck, and he's a damn good meal if you've been giving him corn to get the fishiness out of him. If you shoot him a couple of times a week, you can shoot him the whole season. You've got to pick the right times of day, now. You can't just go down and start blasting away. When I'd be corning a pond, I'd give 'em a little every night. Then when I was ready to shoot, I'd bring only one shell with me. That would keep me from overshooting 'cause you know sometimes it's hard to stop when you get a good thing like that.

To kill ducks, especially the black duck, you've got to bait. There's no getting around it. Trying to sneak up on a duck is just a waste of time. Oh, I've done it down in Dorchester County and usually got my limit too but it's so much easier to bait and better for the birds, too. 'Course, the damn wardens would never see it that way, but I'm sure it kept them stronger and healthier. It only makes sense that if they're well fed and healthy, number one, they'll be able to get back up to their breeding grounds and, number two, they'll have the strength to breed once they get there. Now, don't get me wrong, I never was no market hunter. I killed a lot of ducks in my day, but I very rarely shot over my limit and I *never* sold a duck. Give plenty of 'em away maybe, but never sold one. I'd never go out on a pretty day like today, either, if I was going out. Not many other people was, 'cause it was usually blowing twenty-five to thirty knots out of the northwest. But those of us who did go shot ducks, you can count on that. See, on a stormy day like that a duck knows he's got to fly to eat, and so did we. Then, all you got to do is figure out where he's gonna fly to and be there when he arrives. In other words, you've got to try and think like a duck or a goose which ain't as easy as it sounds.

THERE used to be this old feller, Harry, who lived right across the street. He loved to go hunting, but the poor old guy couldn't see a thing. He was blind as a bat, but we'd take him along ever so often and, man, I mean, you could see on his face how much it meant to him. One real moonlight night we were going out to the cornfields to shoot mallards, and old Harry was with us.

We lay in the fields waiting for the birds to come in, and I'd tell him, "Harry, when you hear me yell 'shoot' to you, get up, and give 'em hell." Well, over they'd come.

"Shoot, Harry," I'd yell. "They're right over us." He'd jump up and bang, bang, bang. He'd shoot the hell out of his old shotgun.

"Did I get any?" he'd ask.

"Sure, you did, Harry. A mess of 'em," I'd tell the old guy.

'Course he never did hit one. But he loved it, and we loved having him.

YOU can't find a better dog for ducking or goose shooting than a Chesapeake. A Chesapeake will freeze another dog to death, if you know what I mean. He'll still be going long after a Lab or any other dog will. I've had my old Chessie with me, ice at least one-eighth of an inch thick on him, and still not refuse a goose I shot. Now, that's something.

I HAD one of them Chesapeakes that could do anything but talk to you, and he'd try that sometimes, too. Now, that ain't all either 'cause you didn't have too much trouble with the game wardens when he was around. That dog could hear a game warden or anybody five miles away against a northwester blowing thirty miles an hour. He was really something. I used to gun in a place down here called Windy Hill. When that tide's really running through there, it's going a good four knots, and after the first outing that dog figured out enough to use that tide to carry him right to a duck. Not only that, but he would dive for cripples, and I mean his whole damn body would disappear. If a duck went under, so did he, and when they came up, they did it together, if you know what I mean.

Watching him bring home a goose was the damndest thing I ever saw. He'd hold that bird around the neck and throw him up over his shoulder onto his back, then swim him in like that. It was the damnest thing I ever saw.

I had him thirteen years and never have seen a better dog. I never did get another one either. I guess it's true what they say about having one truly good one in a lifetime.

You've got to be real careful when you're hunting a new dog around crippled birds, especially geese. They can get damn mean when they want to and hurt a dog pretty good. That's enough to ruin the spirit in some dogs. I was out shootin' coot with a friend of mine once who shot this one bird but didn't kill him, and off the dog went. He was a Chesapeake, too, so keep that in mind. The dog got to the coot and that damn bird started pecking at him like crazy. The dog turned around and come back to the boat without the bird and it took a long time for him to retrieve again, but he did. Remember, I told you he was a Chesapeake.

THAT old Chesapeake Charlie was really something. You know, after a day's hunting I didn't want to pick up no birds so I'd tell him to go retrieve the decoys, sometimes there'd be forty or fifty of them. He'd swim out and back till every damn one of them was brought in, too. Hardly ever would get tangled up in them either.

I've been scared with him, too, though. One morning down at Choptank Light we was gunning in real foul weather. Cold, damp, wind blowing a gale, and he went off after a bird I'd shot. I know I'll never see him again, I thought to myself. Even got that funny feeling in my stomach as I watched him swim off, into the bay, till I couldn't see him no more. See, once he started off after a bird, there was no way you could stop him. He wouldn't listen to nobody then. Things was looking real bad for about an hour till my partner yells, "Hey, look over on the shoreline there," and there was old Charlie coming down the beach to us with that bird thrown over his shoulder just as proud as could be. I was proud of him, too, don't think I wasn't.

ONE Thanksgiving, years ago I was down at my shipyard hanging around with my Chesapeake, Charlie. We wasn't doing any gunning or anything, just waiting for Thanksgiving dinner to be ready so we could go home and eat. Well, as we're sitting there looking over the creek, this old colored woman came down in a rowboat with this big old rooster sitting inside. Guess she was takin' it to cook for her Thanksgiving dinner. Anyway, the bird jumped overboard and with that she started yelling like hell 'cause she couldn't catch the damn thing.

"Mister," she yelled, "can't you do something about gettin' my rooster for me?"

I took Charlie with me down to the wharf, pointed the rooster out to him, and told him to fetch it up. He wouldn't jump off the wharf, but he did run back and down the shoreline till he got right near it. Then he jumped in and swam just as fast as he could to that bird. It was really something to watch when he swam like that. His whole damn body would almost come out of the water, and he'd be paddling and kicking up a wash. Hell, he could swim a canvasback right down. Anyway, Charlie got right up near the bird, circled around him, raised up, and took him right in his mouth. I guess he was a little cautious, 'cause that rooster didn't look like no duck or goose he'd ever seen before. He brought him back into shore alive and unharmed, gave him to me, and I guess that old colored lady had her Thanksgiving dinner after all.

I COULDN'T keep old Charlie in a pit or blind when we was gunning. He'd get so damn excited 'cause he couldn't see what was going on. There'd be no way you could shoot. So I'd put him outside right next to me where I could watch him, and he'd lay there just as calm as could be, scanning the sky.

"Keep looking, Charlie," I'd say to him. "They'll be here."

And, sure enough, they would. He'd see them coming a lot of times before I would. His teeth would start chattering, and he'd look back over at me, I guess just to make sure I saw 'em. Then I'd let 'em have it and off he'd go, swimming like mad to get 'em. The old boy would bring 'em back into the blind soaking wet and, of course, the wetter he was the closer he'd want to get to you, so I'd have to throw him back out again.

AT ONE TIME I rented a one-hundred-acre marsh that I used for my own private gunning, and I discovered the damndest way to bait the birds and shoot 'em. I'd take a small bush like a pine or a cedar and sink it right into the bottom of the river. Then I'd start baiting right around that bush, and I'd have 'em coming in like crazy in no time at all. Then, when I was ready to shoot, I'd move that bush right into range of my blind, and those birds would come right to it looking for the corn. Then, if the wardens should check you, you weren't doing anything wrong. All you was doing was shootin' some real good corn-fed birds.

THAT old Chesapeake of mine was a smart old boy. You could go through this house and open every damn drawer but if you opened the bottom drawer of my bureau his tail would start awaggin' and he'd come right over to you. See, that's where I kept his choker chain, and when he saw that coming out of the drawer, he knew he was going gunning. Hell, he'd even put his head up for you so you could slip that chain on him. When he was twelve years old, he got pretty sick with heartworm and this one day during the season he was home with me and my wife. I didn't gun Charlie no more 'cause he was too old and sick. Anyway, my wife had never seen him work 'cause she never went gunning with us, although she'd heard plenty of stories about him. My son was out that day though and had shot and crippled a goose. He came home and told me about it, and since he didn't have no dog, he was all upset that he wouldn't be able to get it. You know, he thought that poor old goose was gonna have to stay out there, crippled, and die. When he told me this, I said to Charlie, "You want to go one more time, old boy?" and damned if his tail didn't start awaggin'.

I got his choker, and my wife, me, and my son set off with the dog. We got down to that creek. I walked him down to the bank and pointed to where that goose was. He walked into the water and swam about halfway across the creek. Then he stopped and turned around and looked back at me.

"Go on," I yelled to him, and on he went.

When he come back, he had the goose. I almost lost him though. I dried him off and put him in the furnace room to keep his old soul warm, and I told my wife that's the last time he'll ever retrieve, and it was.

Arthur Jones

ARTHUR JONES was born on his family's farm near Cambridge, Maryland, October 3, 1895, one of eight children. A natural hunter and animal lover, he started hunting and dog handling at age eight. A few years later he began taking out hunting parties from the Cambridge Hotel which was run by his father. Among his many clients and friends were Annie Oakley and her husband Frank Butler with whom he did much upland shooting.

In 1921 Jones graduated with the first Maryland State Trooper class and was assigned the motorcycle patrol from Cambridge to Ocean City. Since he did not take much to police work, he left it about one year later to open an automobile repair garage—a business that grew successfully and eventually became a John Deere Farm Equipment Company franchise that today is run by his son and grandson.

Arthur Jones is now widowed and retired, and spends most of his time working in his locally famous gardens, playing with his two dogs, or feeding the ducks in one of the many ponds found around the Cambridge area.

WHEN I was young, our birds were entirely different than the ones you see today. Then, the partridge was a big bird not like the one you see around here now. See, back in the 1920s, the club I did my gunning at started importing birds from Texas 'cause they needed more for their shoots than were available locally. The bird they got was a much smaller bird and able to fly like nothing I'd ever seen before. Where a native bird might fly two hundred-fifty yards, maximum, these damn things could fly half a mile at a clip like it was nothing. And the dogs, they were a lot different too. It seems to me that the pointers and setters we used then were a lot calmer than today's dogs, not nearly as high-strung, and they trained better. Believe me, I know. I've been around and raised dogs my whole life. See, my dad ran the Cambridge Hotel in town and any guests that wanted to go out upland shooting, he'd call me about. I had plenty of places to take them then, 'cause my uncle

62

owned what is now the Blackwater National Wildlife Refuge, and I was really close to him my whole life, so naturally he let me have the run of the place. I'd pick up the hunters in a horse and carriage at the hotel with three or four dogs sitting in the back, and we'd head off down there. We used pointers and setters then and, as I said earlier, they were the most well-behaved dogs you'd ever see.

I'D guide for my uncle, too, a lot of times down at what now is Blackwater National Wildlife Refuge. He had a house out in the middle of the marsh on an island they called Barbados. He rented it for years to a group of about eight millionaires from New York. They'd come down in groups of four on different weekends, and I'd act as their guide sometimes, taking them out to spots, setting up decoys, and working the Chesapeakes. There was also a pond right nearby the house surrounded by reeds about ten feet tall. They'd built a wooden boardwalk to it so you could go down and shoot it if you wanted to. They'd bring beer kegs to sit on, and I'd throw out the decoys till they shot a couple of birds. Then we'd go back to the house. They didn't care too much about shooting really, I don't think. They just wanted to get away and relax. In fact, one of them was a well-known multimillionaire who I never saw go gunning. He'd stay behind to sweep the house, do the dishes and wash, and keep the place up. I thought it was odd then, but now I thoroughly understand it. You see, it's been five years now since I've done any gunning, and I'd love to just be able to go help out around a place like that, swap stories, and be amongst outdoor people—you know, real sportsmen.

THE first time I ever killed a bird I had to walk at least a mile with my dog to get it. I was about ten years old, just a kid, and my older brother had given me one shotgun shell to go out in the field with. I took this old gun we had with a hair trigger and set off with this old bird dog through the fields. He was leaping through the tall grass when he came up on this covey. Up they went, and I shot at them and killed two birds with that one shell. I can still remember how heavy that gun got carrying it through the fields that day, but you know, coming home with those two birds it didn't feel a bit heavy, and, besides, I was so proud I walked the streets so people could see me.

My brother had a Ford dealership here in Cambridge and was all the time entertaining some of the big wigs from Detroit. One time he had a bunch coming down that he knew liked to gun so he figured we'd go out and get them a game dinner, then take them out the next day to do some shootin'.

Well, I was going with him and bringing my Chesapeake who had, by this time, seen his best hunts, if you know what I mean. He had been a hell of a retriever with lots of spirit and still had the desire. It's just that his body was a little old.

We set out that morning, and in no time shot a couple of pheasants that he retrieved. Then off in the distance my brother heard this "honk, honk, honk" coming. Turning to me, he could see I'd heard 'em too.

"Let's get one of them," he said.

All I had with me was some number ten field load, but I put a shell in each barrel, squatted down in the field with my dog, and watched them show up on the horizon. They flew right at me and just as they got in my range I stood up, shot both barrels, and damned if one didn't set his wings and start gliding down.

"Mark him," I yelled to the dog, and we watched that goose glide for at least a thousand feet before he came down. "Fetch it up," I told him, and as tired and feeble as that dog was, off he went to find that goose.

I remember feeling almost sorry for him as he went through that field after the bird, knowing that his best days were behind him. But, damned if he still didn't have the spirit. He brought that goose back and looked up at me with those tired old eyes as I took it from him and patted him on the head. Then we all headed home to clean and cook up the birds. That was his last retrieve—three days later he died in his sleep.

I HUNTED a lot with Annie Oakley and her husband, Frank Butler, when they lived here in Cambridge. She was the quickest, most accurate shot I ever saw, and she pulled that trigger so fast it was impossible to tell how many shots she was getting off. She was just a natural with a gun. See, when she was a young girl, she lost her father, and her mother remarried. Luckily, her stepfather saw the gift she had and encouraged her to stay with it. She told me once that she trained herself not to sight. Taking off her ring, she showed me what she meant. "Now, watch and listen," she said, and each time a bird would fly by, she'd hold that ring out and put it right on the bird. She never led it or nothing, just put it right on target each time. She also learned to shoot for the head so she wouldn't damage the meat.

When I met Annie and Frank it was in their later years, and we used to do a lot of hunting together, especially me and Frank. Most days when he was in Cambridge during the season, me and Frank was out hunting. He was a prince of a man, a pleasure to be with, and could appreciate a good dog working as much as I did.

Now, something happened one day when me and Frank was out hunting that I still kind of feel bad about to this day. We were out in the field with the dogs, and this bird went up. My gun went up and I saw Frank's go up so I didn't shoot. "Bang, bang!" He fired twice and missed! Well, I had my own gun up, and the bird was still in range so I shot at it and killed it.

Not a word was said till we got back to my father's place. Then, when he saw my dad, Frank said to him, "You know, your son did something today that very few people have ever done."

"What's that?" my dad said.

"He shot at and killed a bird after I missed it," and that's all that he said about it.

67

Well, when my dad got me alone, he really laid into me. I'm sure he was afraid I was going to offend him.

"Let it go if it ever happens again," he said. But hell, if it happened today, I'd do the same thing.

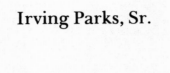

Irving Parks, Sr.

THE lone remaining house on Holland Island, today used as a gun club, was built by the original settler, William A. Parks, in the early 1800s. When his grandson, Irving Parks, Sr., was born there on March 10, 1901, there were approximately three hundred and fifty people settled on the island, all of whom depended on the bay for their living—crabbing, oystering, and fishing in the warmer months and duck hunting and trapping during the colder times.

However, around 1910 the erosion which has adversely affected so many of the islands and shores of the Chesapeake threatened Holland Island as well. Families started leaving, floating their homes on barges to the mainland. It is said that where they eventually settled depended on which way the wind was blowing. Judging by the book *The People of Holland Island,* written and published by Mr. Parks about the history, decline, and resettlement of the people, of Holland Island, this would seem to be true.

In 1918 Mr. Parks's family was forced to leave the island and settle in Cambridge returning for the next seventeen summers until their home was finally washed away.

Mr. Parks remained an active waterman until 1975 when he had to retire because of bad health. He lives today with his daughter in Cambridge.

BACK around 1913 or 1914 we had a man on Holland Island named Major Carroll Todd who trapped black ducks for a living up the bay on Adams Island. He would keep his houseboat up there and stay on it while he was trapping. Then after he would lift a good load of birds he came on back home, barrel them up, and ship them over to Deal Island on the mail boat. Then they would be shipped up to Baltimore to a man named A. D. Sessor who bought most of the birds trapped out there. Back then he got four dollars a pair which was damn good money. Mr. Sessor bought all the blackheads my brother and I trapped in our big traps. Fact is, some years me and my brother would do better trapping ducks than my father would do dredging oysters!

WE had people on Holland Island that completely made their livelihood off of hunting and the bay. It was a great place for shooting ducks and geese and also for trapping otter and mink. They were around all the time. People who lived like that was never broke. They always had some money. They were the greatest people you'd ever see. Seemed like if they got down low on money, they could always go out and catch something and sell it. Then round about the first of March they'd go into the marsh and sound for those diamondback terrapin. See, they'd have a pole about the size of a broomstick and look for a print they'd leave in the mud about the size of a horseshoe. Then they'd take that stick and push it down into the mud right on that horseshoe, and if you heard a hollow thumping sound, it meant that at least one was down there. Sometimes you could get as many as five or six from one spot by poling them and digging down with your hands.

You sold them by the inch, the size of their shells. Up to five inches was one dollar, six inches was three-fifty and anything over that would fetch around four to four-fifty which was a good bit of money then.

WHEN I was young and coming up on Holland Island we used to set these duck traps to catch blackheads. See, back then you had a right to trap 'em and ship 'em into Baltimore. Nobody would bother you 'cause there was no laws against it.

We set our traps out west of Holland Island in the bay at a place called Bay Shore Ridge. These was a little different than the traps they set for black ducks out in the marshes of Smith Island. They stood about six or seven feet above the bay, held together with poles that were stuck into the bottom about four feet and totally wrapped in chicken wire. They were about sixty feet long, set in a horseshoe shape with a funnel at one end. We'd bait them with a corn and wheat mixture that my

74

father would buy for us up the Nanticoke River at Lewis Wharf. See, we didn't have enough land on the island to grow corn for baitin' so we had to go off and buy it. After we had the trap baited, we'd usually put about a half dozen decoys inside it and go sit on the shore in a blind or a shanty and watch what was going on through a pair of glasses. Just as soon as the flocks would break up and go into the trap and we were sure we had a good enough catch inside, we'd sneak out and close off the funnel. Sometimes you'd have one hundred and fifty to two hundred blackheads inside. Then we'd open up the tops in spots and scoop out the birds with crab nets, pack them in sacks, and get 'em ready to ship. Now to ship them we either had to bring them over to Deal Island which was eight miles away, or sometimes we could put them on the mail boat that went over in the evenings. Then the Deal Island boys would ship them to Baltimore. You could make yourself a pretty good buck with a good day's catch. Sometimes they'd pay us a dollar a piece for them, and never less than fifty cents a head. There was this one old fellow, my father's uncle, who would take five from us every time we went out as soon as we got back to the dock. He loved to eat those blackheads and would sometimes cook 'em two at a time for himself. We always charged him a dollar for the five of them. He was a good old soul.

I REMEMBER four of those big guns out on Holland Island at one time. They'd carry a pound of powder, a pound of shot, and use rope wadding. Took two men to carry them down to the skiffs usually. They was so damn big. They'd sneak up on the flocks in those skiffs and sometimes they would really slaughter them. I saw my uncle kill a hundred and eighty some canvasbacks in one shot once. His gun was passed down from *his* grandfather so you can see how long that one had been around.

My grandfather was blind ten or twelve years before he died, and I used to go up and sit with him many a night at his place and listen to the four of them shoot those big guns. They'd usually go out together, and when they went off all at once, that sound rolled across the bay like a deep thunder. It was really something. Now, when the wind was northeast before a storm and they'd shoot, my grandfather would tell me to go down around Duck Island shore and that's where the cripples would be and sure enough next morning there'd be cripples rafted up and usually a few dead birds.

YOU know that picture in *The Outlaw Gunner** of all the men standing in front of the picket fence on Holland Island? Well, one of them was my uncle. They was all fishermen who was waiting around for the weather to moderate so they could go out and set their nets when this man come by who was a photographer and got them all to pose for him.

They'd set the gill nets out in the bay for "tailers" (bluefish, you'd call them). They'd catch a mess of them, small ones around a pound, pound and a half, and the little bit they got for 'em back then was what they lived on.

The Outlaw Gunner by Harry M. Walsh (Centreville, Maryland: Tidewater Publishers, 1971).

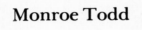

Monroe Todd

BORN at Crocheron, Maryland, December 9, 1913, Monroe Todd has spent his entire life in this quiet bayfront community. A waterman all his adult years, Todd has also acted as a guide at the Bishop's Head Gun Club until recently when pressure from wardens forced him to give it up to become the club's caretaker.

Todd and his twelve-year-old Chesapeake, Chief, can be found crabbing on the bay each day during the season. On off days they are at home with Stella, Monroe's wife of forty-nine years.

WHEN I first got married I was crazy about gunnin'. See, we could kill all the ducks we wanted then, bait, and do what we pleased. But when you stop baiting ducks they just ain't fit to eat. They used to catch them here in duck traps and ship 'em to Baltimore. Lots of people made their living from it. Then they outlawed trapping and baiting. Then the limits come down gradually to where it is now. One damn black duck a day. Can you imagine that? Why, back then, if you had just one duck you'd be so embarrassed you'd throw it in the marsh rather than come home with one. I can remember seeing big bunches of ducks hanging in peoples' breezeways, keeping cool just waiting to get shipped.

Then the government come in and really put the stop to all that and, boy, did they foul everything else up in the meantime. You can't shoot a duck or goose, trap a muskrat or a raccoon out of that preserve now. What the hell good is it?

ONE Christmas Eve years ago me and a couple of my buddies was rigged out for geese in a blind we kept on the Nanticoke River. It was a great spot for gunning geese—water on one side and a big cornfield that the birds fed in on the other. Anyway, it was getting toward dusk. It was cold. Snow was on the ground, in the air, and wind blowing hard. We were going to make sure that we brought home the Chrismas goose that year so we brought one of those portable record players that were used for calling in ducks and geese with us. We had it set up and calling real pretty when in come a flock of nine birds— they set their wings and started coming in, and we let 'em have it, killing all nine. Just then this damn warden appears out of nowhere from behind the blind. Taps me on the shoulder and says, "Say, would you mind telling me what that is you're playing on the record player?"

"Well, I wish it were 'White Christmas,'" I answered, "but it isn't."

That was a real expensive Christmas—cost each one of us five hundred dollars and a year's hunting probation.

LET me tell you a story about my Chesapeake, Chief. I'll cook for him every morning—not one morning—every morning, three slices of beef. Then I'll go off crabbing and bring him with me. Now, I'm carrying three sandwiches for myself and three for him and when I eat one, I'll give him one. That's the dog's life for you! For dinner he'll have some chicken or leftover slices of beef. He won't eat dog food. He'll eat pork, beef, and chicken, but he don't care for no dog food. He loves ice cream, though. Now, for a snack I'll carry an orange with me usually, and when I get time I sit down and peel the orange and he'll eat it with me.

But chicken's what he loves best. Every Saturday I'll go down to the store and buy him a chicken. My wife cleans it up and cooks it for him with our dinner on Sunday, and every Sunday he'll eat at least half of that for his dinner.

I HAD this old gunnin' friend of mine, Josh, that I used to go with quite a bit before he passed away. He was quite a character, old Josh. I remember this one time just after Josh had started shootin' ducks. He was to have a bunch of company over for dinner that next day so he decided he was going out that morning and kill himself a load of ducks to feed 'em. Now, somebody had pointed out a redbreasted merganser to him at one time and told him it was called water pheasant which it is down in these parts, but what they neglected to tell him was how damn fishy tastin' they are. See, they feed on fish, piss clams, and mussels, and that taste gets right through them. You know you can't even bait one of them birds with corn like you can most birds. They'd just rather eat fish! But the name's what got Josh and he thought like a land pheasant they must be real good eatin'.

Josh went out that morning and killed himself three water pheasants (sheldrakes, water witches, or sawbills which they're also called), one canvasback, and two scaup or broadbills. He was real happy with himself carrying them home that morning. When he came home he got one of the local colored women to clean and come over and cook 'em for him. And as she was cookin' those birds up outside, people that lived around him was actually comin' round the house to see if something was burning! Needless to say, that dinner turned out to be a total disaster, and when Josh told me the whole story about a month later, I told him straight-faced as could be, "Gee, Josh. I can't understand it. You must have had them cooked wrong."

"Yeah, yeah. That's what I thought," he said leaning up on the table to get closer to me.

"You can't let them lay in their own juices," I said. "You've got to get yourself a piece of soft balsa wood about one inch thick, tack the bird to it with brass tacks so it don't rust, then put it in a covered pot with water in the bottom. Keep basting

87

him with his own juices mixed in with the water, but don't let him lay in it. Then, when you're satisfied that the bird is cooked, untack him from the wood, throw the bird away, bring the balsa wood inside, cut it in small pieces, and serve it!"

WE'D shoot black ducks over bait at dusk down near St. Pierre Island. Unless a damn duck has been corn fed it ain't worth a damn. In fact, I'd rather eat a raw hot dog and I have, too, before I'd eat any duck that hadn't been fed on corn.

We'd corn 'em usually for about two weeks, puttin' out a quart or so in the same area every other day. The bottom is real muddy around St. Pierre Island, and when you were wading around baiting spots, you could feel if they were eating by whether or not the kernels was still in the mud. I don't know how long those black ducks can stretch their necks, but it must be a good amount 'cause they'd usually get every damn bit of bait.

After about a week or so, we' start looking for signs to see if their meat was getting good from the corn. See, if the wind was blowing northwest, all their preening feathers would get washed up on the shoreline, and we'd go down and look for them and any droppings that might be around. If the feathers were fresh, you could see the faintest sign of oil around them from the corn, or if you saw the droppings was a yellow color, then you knew the meat was getting right and that's when we'd shoot them.

Now, the best way to shoot them is to sit and wait for them to come into the bait, then when they pitch in towards it, let them have it. See, this way they're gonna fall in the river, and you know right where they are. If you shoot 'em over a marsh or if they fall in there you might as well forget it, 'cause without a dog you're never gonna find 'em. I've stood and marked the exact spot where I saw a bird go down, never take my eye off it, and send Josh after it. He'd go right to the spot and never could find it. But, next morning, if you brought somebody's dog, he'd lead you right to it 'cause by that time either the raccoons or crows would eat the breast meat out of 'em and they wouldn't be worth a damn.

89

We had two concrete blinds down in the Manokin River near St. Pierre Island that we used almost all the time for shootin'. Far as I know parts of them are still there today. We'd always face our blinds with the backs to the northwest, to keep 'em out of the prevailing west winds that you get in the winter.

Sometimes we'd be sitting there with a rig of decoys set out in front of us, and you could start to see ice forming on one of the decoy's bills. Then in no time at all, the bird would start to get covered with ice and disappear below the surface from the weight. But you could always see little ripples in the water where they went down so I'd go out in my skiff to that spot, and all you could see would be a bushel-basket-sized piece of mushy ice just below the surface. Now I'd take my oar and give it a good shot on the top and with that all the ice would break off, and the decoy would pop right back up dry. "Comin' up dry" we called it.

Another thing we did in those rigs was to rig ourselves a decoy to dive from a little cord in the blind. We had an old dipper decoy that was painted up like a drake goldeneye (whistler). We'd tie one end of that to the decoy, run it through the hole in a piece of concrete block, and into the blind. I'd cut a small hole in the front of the blind with a wood chisel and had that line right there where I could get to it. We'd wait till a drake goldeneye would fly over the rig, then I'd pull right hard on that line, and the decoy would go under head first. And, almost every time the bird would pitch right into the spot where the decoy disappeared and wait, which is really something 'cause it's been my experience that those drake goldeneyes are real shy. Anyway, that bird would sit there a little while, then dive right after the decoy. But, he must have realized what was going on, 'cause when they came up, they came up flying. They'd hit the surface and just keep right on going so you'd have to shoot 'em right as they came out of the water.

91

I NEVER sold a duck in my life! Didn't eat that many of them either, but I never made one red cent off of selling them. Most of the birds that I shot I gave away to friends or families that I knew was hurtin' and could use them. Hell, if you had me over for a meal and you was serving wild ducks I'd ask you if you had a raw hot dog instead 'cause unless they was corn fed they're not worth a damn.

Back in 1940, my father had an old four-cylinder Model A truck that I would drive back and forth to the markets in Washington, Baltimore, and New York. One time I made five trips to the New York market in seven days with her, and, man, let me tell you that's a lot of driving. We was hauling oysters from all over the Eastern Shore. At least, that's what I was told. Then my dad got a contract to haul oysters for this man in Crisfield. They were in one-gallon sealed containers which made me a little suspicious 'cause usually oysters just have the lids pressed on. But I ran them anyway.

It turned out I was right 'cause I found that each one-gallon container had two trapped black ducks from Smith Island in 'em. Christ, if they had caught me doing that I still might be doing time. But, that's the only money I ever made off ducks.

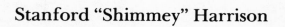

Stanford "Shimmey" Harrison

Born on Deal Island, Maryland on October 6, 1911, Stanford "Shimmey" Harrison grew up on the bay, fishing and hunting.

An oyster tonger for awhile, he also ran a service station on Deal Island before turning to guiding and caretaking full time. He worked first for the Wayne Pump Company and then for the Bound family, owners of Holland Island until recently. Today Shimmey lives on Deal Island with his wife Bea and his flock of tame Canada geese.

YOU must have seen that book out now that was written by that head warden, Willie Parker?* Hell, I even had a run-in with him one time. It was opening week of the gunning season and Mr. Bounds called me to take him over to the island and go fishing. Now, we was going fishing, had nothing at all to do with gunning, you understand. Me and the other guide and Mr. Bounds left the dock and headed out towards Adams Island up near Holland Island. We stayed awhile and caught a few fish there.

The tide was right, and I said, "Mr. Bounds, how about going down to the island and trolling around the channel?"

"Good enough," he said, and we headed back to Holland where in no time at all we caught four or five six-pound rock, a bluefish, and something so damn big that about two-thirds of the way in, it snapped the line and got away. We worked our way, trolling down to the southwest end of the island, and I could see this other boat trolling off in the distance.

"Mr. Bounds," I said, "I think that's the game warden. He must've thought we were out here ducking."

We headed out towards the boat, and as we got up on her I could make out the man running the boat. It was Mr. Badget, a warden but a fine gentleman. He had a job to do, and he was just adoin' it. They went around, and we followed behind 'em still making believe like we was trolling when I spotted another little runabout with a cabin on it making believe like it was fishing, too. But, hell, I could tell from the way he looked and where he was sitting that he didn't care about catching no fish. At the same time, I could see the other boat pull up near to one of our blinds and stop.

"They're waiting for us now, Mr. Bounds," I said.

With that, the runabout came alongside of us, and a man in it says to Mr. Bounds, "I assume you're Mr. Bounds."

"Yes, I am," he answered.

*Game Warden: Chesapeake Assignment by Willie J. Parker (Centreville, Maryland: Tidewater Publishers, 1983).

"I'm Willie Parker," he replied.

Well, I jumped right in and introduced myself and the other guide, and with that, Parker announced:

"This baitin' has got to stop right away."

"We're not throwing any bait over," I told him.

But he replied, "There are fifteen hundred ducks in Holland Strait, and you've got 'em all staying right around here."

Now, that was a damn lie, and it made me angrier than hell and I told him so, too.

"There haven't been more than fifty ducks out here till this northwest wind blew up," I told him in no uncertain terms! And, damn it, I knew 'cause I was out there every day. I kept an eye on what was goin' on. Mr. Bounds and him talked a while longer and before I knew it, we were all headed back to the clubhouse to have coffee, sandwiches, and a nice chat, too. They left finally, I guess satisfied that they'd done their job although they hadn't caught us doing anything, and hell, they was a real nice bunch of people, too. But, like I said before, they just had a job to do. Just pissed me off with that attitude about the fifteen hundred ducks 'cause I knew he didn't know what he was talking about.

WE were out gunning one morning during goose season and this black duck and teal come right into us. So, we killed 'em both, sent out our retrievers, sat back, and waited for more birds to come in. All of a sudden I heard this "knock, knock, knock" from the back of the blind, but I didn't pay it no attention 'cause the wind was blowing about twenty-five to thirty miles an hour out of the northwest and I was sure it was just something banging up against the back.

Then I heard it again, and this time somebody announced from outside, "Open up, it's the warden!" and damned if it wasn't two federal men. "Well, boys, whose are those two ducks you just shot?"

Well, I just about shit. We'd put 'em up on top of the blind, so I answered, "Two ducks, now, what two ducks you talking about?"

He looked through the blind, went outside up on the roof, and I heard him say, "Well, look what we have here. I guess you don't know nothing about these?" and at that point we knew we'd had it and didn't even answer. But after a couple of awkward minutes, the two gunners we had with us told the wardens that they'd done the shootin'. One came over to me, looked at my gun, and asked me if it was loaded.

"Yes, it is," I told him, "but I'm only out here to shoot cripples for these fellows if they need it."

I guess he didn't buy that 'cause he gave me a ticket for aiding and abetting, and I had to go up to Cambridge to pay the fine.

W AY back you used to get your limit most every day you went. The times I'm thinking of was before they had more wardens in the marshes than ducks, and it seems like that sometimes now. Back then, the wardens would come down here usually once a year in a big boat called *The Loon.* They'd show up and anchor in some creek, come ashore in little boats, and look around seeing if they could find anything illegal going on. Well, you'd have to of been a real damn fool to do anything with that big boat sittin' out there in the first place. You know they wasn't exactly being undercover. After a while they'd pull up their anchor and head over to Smith Island or sit in Holland Strait for a couple of days. But every once in a while they'd pull up to the dock area on Deal Island and I'd go down, talk to 'em, and ask 'em questions. For instance, I told 'em I had a lot of muskrat traps out after the season and every once in a while I'd catch myself a black duck in one of them. I wanted to know what was I supposed to do with that dead duck. Well, they told me it was against the law to kill or possess a dead duck out of season and that's all the advice they could give me. I thanked them for it and went right on bringing those dead ducks home to eat. But, like I said before, and even now somewhat, I guess, they just had a job to do and was doing it. You've got to remember most of this happened before there was so much pressure on them to start coming down on people for killing and especially trapping which was real hard on the birds. Besides, most of the wardens then was real outdoors men, not like you got today. Christ, most of the wardens today never been inside a blind in their life.

99

Captain Alex Kellam

CAPTAIN ALEX KELLAM was born on Smith Island at Rhodes Point on October 9, 1908. He lived there, working as a waterman and gunning until the time when his daughter was ready to enter high school. At that time, Smith Island children who went to high school had to go across the bay to Crisfield and stay with a family in town during the weeks school was in session, only coming home on vacations and weekends. Feeling that a girl should be with her family during those years, Kellam and his wife sold their home on Smith Island and moved to Crisfield to begin a new way of life. Kellam took a job with a local insurance company where he worked for twenty years until retirement. He still lives today in Crisfield with his wife.

A born storyteller, Capt. Kellam would always draw a crowd when he started spinning yarns about life on Smith Island and the Chesapeake Bay. This natural talent of the raconteur evolved into a part-time occupation. He travels around the East Coast speaking at various community benefits, and he has been a featured speaker at the Smithsonian Institution's Folklore and Arts Festivals.

As a close friend of the late Ward brothers, Lem and Steve, the famous decoy carvers, Kellam sat and swapped stories with them for hours. It was during this time that Steve, also a gifted poet, would recite his work which dealt with life on the Chesapeake Bay. In his colorful stories Captain Kellam incorporated two of Steve Ward's many poems as well as two others by unknown Eastern Shore poets, one of them a Lem Ward favorite.

THERE was a man here years ago named Alec Howard. He used to ship ducks and sell bootleg whiskey. One day this undercover government man come up to him and said, "I hear you can get me a pint of whiskey."

"I can," Alec says.

"Well, I'd like you to get me a pint."

So Alec says, "All right, you give me two dollars and hold this package for me, and I'll be right back."

So the government man give him the money and off Alec went.

Well, that government man waited and waited and waited, but old Alec never came back. So, figuring that maybe Alec wasn't comin' back with his two dollars, but at least he had his package, the government man opened it up, and there was the whiskey!

I REMEMBER one real pretty moonlit night, me and this buddy of mine, Charlie Marsh, was up at Mussel Hole lighting the geese. Charlie, or Pooky, as we called him, and me killed three or four right away with the lantern and was headed back up through a creek in our skiff when I saw three men off in the distance poling towards us in a boat. Luckily, I saw them first 'cause I knew right away they was game wardens. We pushed our boat right under the vent on the edge of the creek and lay down flat. The vent is the edge of the shoreline that will hang over from the water beating into it and eating it away. Kinda makes like a roof over your head when you're laying there under it.

Anyway, we lay there for what seemed like hours till these three wardens pushed by us in their skiff. As they was coming by, I could hear one of them say, "They're down here. I'm sure I heard a gun go off." We stayed right down in our skiff till we were pretty sure that they was gone. Then we pulled ourselves out and headed back up the creek. On the way, we stopped and shot six more geese, right under their noses. Figuring they

heard these shots, too, we put the birds in the skiff and hid it real good in some reeds. Then we walked down the bay side beaches and doubled back to the boat to see if they were around or not. The boat looked like it hadn't been touched so we pulled it out, jumped in, and come on home with the birds.

NOT too long after that night lighting geese up at Mussel Hole, Pooky and me went out looking for geese on the bars with my big gun, Burnsides, and Pooky's automatic. We come up on this flock off on a bar, and before I knew what was happening, Pooky switched the boat side to and started firing his automatic. I picked up my big gun, put it to my shoulder, and touched her off. I cut a path right through 'em, killing three. "Christ," Pooky yelled, "you killed 'em, and I couldn't even get shot to 'em with my automatic. Next time, let's load her right up full and really let 'em have it."

I wasn't crazy about the notion, but the idea of killing a load of geese sounded real good. So, next night we set out again, with the Burnsides loaded chock full. We found ourselves another flock, but couldn't get right up close on 'em, 'cause there was too much moonlight. They must have seen us 'cause they started to fly. With that, Pooky yells, "Shoot 'em, damn it. Shoot 'em!"

I picked her up, put her up, and touched her off again. And, you know, she knocked me and Pooky overboard, before we knew what hit us, into about two feet of water and, man, let me tell you, that water was cold! We scrambled around for a while, got back in the boat, which luckily wasn't damaged, neither was Pooky, but, Christ, did I hurt—my eyes was black, ear drums busted, and teeth chattering, and no damn birds to show for it that night.

HERE'S one of Steve Ward's poems, written about fifty years ago, that I like to recite.

All That I Ask

Give me a wind-swept storm beaten coast, pounded and lashed
>   by the gale—
>   Watching the winging feathered host, the speck of an off
>   shore sail
Hearing the song of wild geese at night wafting their way
>   from afar.
>   With naught to guide them in their flight, only the ray
>   of a star—
Give me the roar of tumbling sea, upon a thundering shore:
>   And this is all I'll ask of thee, and why should I ask for
>   more?
There in a shanty, bathed in moon-beams, reflected by water's
>   blue
>   Is all that I ask, lost in dreams for ever and ever with you.

THIS was a favorite poem of the Ward brothers, but nobody knows who wrote it.

A faithful dog will play with you, laugh with you, and cry.
Starve just to stay with you for no reason why.
When you're feelin' out of sorts, somehow they understand.
They'll look at you with their shiny eyes and try and understand.
Their blind, implicit faith is bound only by their love, which we
  should all have for our master up above.
And after all is said and done, I guess this isn't odd.
When you spell dog backwards, you get the name God.

I NEVER knew anybody to get hurt bad with a punt gun. See, there was one thing that those old gunners knew. As long as you used the charger like you was supposed to, not overloaded with powder, one eight-gauge shell full of powder and one of shot, that was enough, and you didn't have enough charge to do any damage. It was when you overloaded her that you'd run into problems. Then she got real dangerous. I remember one night I was out huntin' with this feller, and he said, "I want two loads of powder in her."

Well, I loaded her that way, reluctantly, of course. Luckily, she was lashed down pretty good 'cause when he touched her off she ripped the whole bow out of that skiff. It would've killed him if it got loose. He got his five geese with her, though. He come aboard later, laughing.

"Damn, it's a good thing you had her lashed down good," he roared. I'm just glad I wasn't aboard the skiff when he shot her.

THEY tell this story about this old feller. His name was Joe Cluart. But they called him Joe Sour. He lived up at a place called Mussel Hole. Your chart will show it as South Marsh Island, a great gunnin' spot. It was snowin' to beat hell one day, the wind blowing out of the north about twenty miles an hour. Now he was in Mitten Creek on the east side of Mussel Hole and the brant, geese, and ducks was "corded up" in there. There were so many of them Joe skiffed right up on 'em, pointed that bow of his boat with the big gun right at 'em, and yelled at the top of his lungs, "Joe Sour's gonna clean the bar."

With that, up went the birds which, of course, he wanted. He slapped down the trigger, and off she went with a roar, pushing that boat back eight to twelve feet as they did when those big guns went off. Well, when he picked up his head to look, there wasn't a damn thing on the water, not one dead bird. Now, he didn't miss much, in fact, never, so to say he was dumbfounded was puttin' it mildly. But 'cause it was blowin' and snowin' so bad he knew that the birds wouldn't fly far, and he poled off to another cove where he figured they might be stopping. On the way, he stopped in some deep water bushes to load his gun again. When he picked up his shot bag, it was still full of the shot that he'd forgot to load in the gun before.

AFTER those big guns would go off, there'd be a lot of people who aimed to be down on the beaches next mornin' to pick up cripples. The brant cripples would always drift up together and that's how you'd find 'em. A goose will get under the water with just his bill out and at night he's hard to see.

I was ahuntin' up at Mussel Hole one day with my double-barreled gun and in come five geese, pitchin' towards the cove where I was rigged out. There was a gander, three goslings, and the mother goose which I never even thought about. I just wanted to get all five of them. So, when they got abreast of me and crossed necks, I let them have it with both barrels and killed three. The other two took off, flew a couple of hundred yards around, and pitched back to the others. By this time, I'd reloaded both barrels and shot them, too. And, man, I'll tell you I was pretty proud of myself. No remorse or anything. Then one day I was reading William Warner's book, *Beautiful Swimmers,* and I came across this poem by Truman P. Reatmeyer.

Remorse

A hunter shot at a flock of geese
That flew within his reach.
Two were stopped in their rapid flight
And fell on the sandy beach.
The male bird lay at the water's edge
And just before he died
He faintly called to his wounded mate
And she dragged herself to his side.
She bent her head and crooned to him
In a way distressed and wild
Caressing her one and only mate
As a Mother would her child.
Then covering him with her broken wing
And gasping with failing breath
She laid her head against his breast,
A feeble honk . . . then death.
This story is true, though crudely told,
I was the man in the case.
I stood knee deep in the drizzle and cold
And the hot tears burned my face.
I buried the birds in the sand where they lay
Wrapped in my hunting coat,
And I threw my gun and belt in the Bay
When I crossed in the open boat.
Hunters will call me a right poor sport
And scoff at the thing I did;
But that day something broke in my heart,
And shoot again? God forbid!

That took me right back to the day on Mussel Cove and, man, it really upsets me now.

HERE'S what I think was the last poem that Steve Ward wrote:

The Drifter

I'm just an old has-been decoy,
    no ribbons have I won.
My sides and head are full of shot
    from many a blazing gun.
My home is down on the river,
    driftin' along with the tide.
No roof have I for shelter,
    no one place I can abide.
I've rocked to the winter's wild fury,
    I've scorched from the heat of the sun.
I've drifted and drifted and drifted,
    the tide never ceased to run.
I was picked up by some fool collector
    and put up on the shelf.
But my home is down by the river
    when I can drift all by myself.
I long to go back to the shoreline
    where the clouds are thick and low.
And feel the touch of the raindrops
    and the velvet soft touch of the snow.

BEFORE the days of marine railways in Crisfield, people would get together, sometimes ten or fifteen of them at a time, and pull their boats up on the beaches together to work on or paint the bottoms. Now, if it was too cold one day they all might get together in one of the old seine houses or stores in town to sit and talk. I can smell that copper paint now around the first day of crabbin'. You could look out over those creeks and see hundreds of those sailboats sittin' there ready to go out. Steve Ward wrote a poem that describes it better than anybody ever could. It goes:

It is soft crab time in Crisfield, you can hear the hammers ring;
They are fitting up the skip-jacks, it's the first sure sign of spring.
Bottoms all red with copper, sides are white and washboards drab;
Sails of snowy white are streaming; it's the time for Crisfield crabs.

You can hear the hoops go ringing, for they go up mighty fast;
You can hear the halyard singing in the wind beside the mast;
You can hear the crab gulls chatter, as they circle, dip, and scream;
For it's soft crab time in Crisfield—soft crabs from the Crisfield
        streams.
Yes, it's soft crab time in Crisfield, and it brings a world of dreams
To go skimming o'er the water on a June night's moonlit stream.
It is springtime in the woodlands where all nature seems to rhyme,—
It is summer in the meadows, and in Crisfield, SOFT CRAB TIME!

WE had this federal warden once on Smith Island who flew a seaplane all the time, checking up on what was goin' on. His name was something like Leon D. Cool. Well, he was a real smart ass. Used to land his plane, come into the villages, and stir everybody up. Get 'em real mad.

I went to him one time and said, "I'd like to offer you a piece of advice," I said. "You're making a mistake, coming ashore and agitating these people. You're makin' them damn mad and making things worse on yourself. If you're not careful, someone's liable to find you in one of those crab holes. You know, it's one thing to do your job in the world, but stay the hell out of town," I told him. Well, like I said, he was a smart ass.

"I can take care of myself," he said to me all high and mighty.

"No doubt you can," I said, "and there's plenty of them that can take care of you, too," I said and walked away.

Now this went on and he kept stoppin' in the villages, stirring people up. Till one Sunday he was flyin' around and spotted this trap in the marsh over at the end of Rhodes Point. He landed the plane as close as he could to it, got out, and walked up to the trap. Well, just as he got up on that trap this voice came across the marsh real clear.

"You put your hands on that trap and you're a dead man," and with that the smart ass bowed in the direction of the voice and just as he bent over, one of those .45-.70 caliber balls hit the water right in front of him and splashed up water all over him. On his ass he went, not 'cause he was hit. He was just startled as hell. Needless to say, he stopped. He got up and started back to his plane and damned if another bullet didn't land right next to him. He speeded up a little, you might say, and just as he got to his plane, another went off. Well, by now you can imagine how scared he was. He reached into the plane and pulled out a carbine. By now there were fifteen or twenty people standing watching this whole thing from town and the warden thought one of them was doin' the shootin', but they wasn't. It was comin' from the attic of a house and I know 'cause I know who was doin' it. Anyway, he put that carbine up to his shoulder, pointing it towards the crowd and that voice said to him, "You pull that trigger and it'll be the last thing you ever do."

Well, he put that rifle back in the plane, jumped in right behind it, and took off out of there. Then, 'cause of this whole thing, we had FBI agents all over the place for a couple of months, and although they had a pretty good idea who done it and they was right, they never were able to pin it on him. But you know, somebody finally did kill the bastard down around Currituck after that. He just never learned his lesson.

WHEN I got married, my mom said, "I hate to see you leave this family. You've been a good provider of ducks and fish for us." You see, I was always trapping or shootin' birds and when it was warmer, catchin' fish.

I remember the first time I ever trapped real serious. I'd set my traps out, had 'em baited with corn, and every time I'd check the damn things, all the corn would be eaten up to the door and there it would stop. So, after havin' this go on a couple of days, it started to really bother the hell out of me so I sat right there to see just what the hell was goin' on and damned if the sea gulls wasn't eatin' it all up. Now, a sea gull can't digest corn so what they'd do is load up on it and when they'd gorged themselves, they'd fly over to a sand bar and spit it all up. I bet I found a half bushel on one bar alone. I straightened that problem out right away to the dismay of four sea gulls who I'll guarantee you never ate corn or anything else for that matter again. I busted the hell out of them and the next morning I had ten or fifteen ducks in there, and they were fat as they could be. We'd always use corn to bait 'em. They loved it more than anything, and after they ate it for a week, man, did they taste good. Especially the black duck. Once they see that you got corn out, they'll come in like crazy but not till after dark. They're smart bastards. Sometimes we'd even bait a pond or water hole and on a stormy night wait for them to come in and shoot the hell out of 'em.

WHEN I was a young boy, my father would send me down to Tylerton to buy ducks to eat. They'd be hanging right on the side of Marshall's store. Tylerton was a famous spot around here for market hunting. I'll bet there were twenty guns out there back in the 1930s, and all of those guns had names. The gun that I used later on was a number four. You could shoot her from the shoulder, but when you come up with her you had to take aim quick 'cause she was heavy and if you over-loaded her, Rocky Marciano or Dempsey couldn't hit you any harder than she would kick you. Mostly, I'd lash her to a skiff and use her that way. I'd tie and chock her down and put bags of sea grass behind the stock to take up the recoil. Then I'd lie right beside her and use the hand paddles to get me up in range of the birds, and, let me tell you, anytime you could skiff up on a flock of wild geese you was doing something right 'cause they're always on the lookout too. We'd shoot at different times of the day. One of them was the last glow of daylight in the evening or the first glow in the morning or high moon—south moon, they called it. My first time there were four of us out there—Capt. Willie Marshall, Capt. Watson Marshall, Lawrence Marshall, and myself. I had the Burnsides with me. That's what I called my gun. She was made over in England where all the one piece tapered barrel guns was made. Anyway, it was a full moon that night and Capt. Willie said, "We'll wait till the moon is directly overhead." He called it a south moon. "Till we skiff up on 'em and shoot." And that's what we did. We shot and killed forty-eight brant and none of 'em flew, so we got them all. Now, just before we shot I'd looked behind me and I couldn't tell the difference between the water and the sky. It was all blended together and later I asked Capt. Willie why he waited till then, about midnight, when the moon was directly overhead, to shoot. He told me 'cause then there was no reflections in the water and damned if he wasn't right.

119

As a boy I used to take my old single barrel and go down to the creeks to watch the king divers (goldeneye) diving. I'd count 1, 2, 3, 4,—till they come up, then watch 'em dive again, and count. One day I had nine shells with me and that was a ton, you know, back then, 'cause you were lucky if you had two usually. Anyway, I'd sit there watching this duck dive and countin'. Then when he come up this one time—boom! I'd let him have it and under he'd go. You know, they can duck you like nothing—"dive at a flash," we called it. I shot eight of my shells at him doin' that. Had one left and I said to myself, "I'm not wasting that one on him." Well, up he come and for some reason took right off aflyin'. So, I let him have it, and down he come. Took all my shells to get that bugger, but I finally did.

W<small>E'D</small> shoot geese mostly back in the creeks where they'd feed at night, but it was hard, real hard, to sneak up on 'em. Like I said before, they always had their sentries who was on the lookout when the others was feedin', and they'd scatter out so it would make it harder to kill a bunch with one shot. And then, most times, you'd have the pintails feedin' right behind them so if they heard you comin' and took off, so would the geese. The most I ever heard being shot was ninety and that was with two shots. See, every day a goose has got to go out to the sand bars after feeding and get a little bit of that sand in his gizzards to help him digest his food. So that's what we'd do, we'd watch them for a couple of days, sometimes feedin', and see where they'd go to get the sand. Then we'd go out to that spot and shoot 'em.

THERE was a fellow down here that had a dog that would come back from a pond or the bay and bark to tell you how many ducks was there.

One day he had a relative from the city visiting him and he told him about his dog and what he could do. 'Course the city feller didn't believe one word of it so the man heeled his dog and told him to go out back to the pond and check it for ducks. Off he went and a short time later he come back and barked twice.

"That means there's two ducks out there," the fellow said to the city man.

"That's amazing," he said. "Let's see him do it again."

So he sent the dog out to the creek and out he went, comin' back and barking three times.

"I don't believe it," said the city man. "Send him down to the river and let's see what he does."

And off the dog went to the river. Now after about a half hour he returned carrying a stick and shaking like he'd seen a ghost.

City man says, "What's he doing now?"

"He's telling you that there's more ducks down there than you can shake a stick at!"

Isaac Lankford

Photo: Chesapeake Bay Maritime Museum

BORN January 21, 1891, in the Crisfield area, Isaac Lankford was one of the few people in this country to perfect the method of making the punt guns used by market hunters on the Chesapeake Bay. He had made about fifty of these guns when federal agents paid him a visit one day and informed him it might be in his best interest to stop making them.

A carpenter and decoy carver most of his life, Isaac was also a waterman and a hunter, especially when the craving for a duck dinner struck him.

He lives today with his wife Ruth across the street from where he was born.

I HAD a four-barreled gun mounted on the bow of a little skiff that I'd used for gunning.

Now, usually, when we'd go out, there'd be three boats together. Two set up to shoot ducks and one pointin' to the rear to shoot wardens if they showed up. We never had to do that, but I'm sure if the need arose we would of.

One day about fifty years ago, I headed out of the creek by myself into Pocomoke Sound towards Cedar Strait which was generally a good feeding spot for the birds. On my way out I kept passing all kinds of ducks especially them little baldpates and I got to thinking that maybe this was going to be a real good night. When I got up near the strait, I saw the most ducks and brant I'd ever seen rafted up, hundreds and hundreds of them sitting on that bay. Carefully, I skiffed up to within range

128

of them and waited there quietly until the sun had just gone down far enough and the sky was red. Then I slowly reached for the trigger string and to this day I don't remember pulling it. I was out at least four or five hours I guess, and when I woke up, my skiff was bangin' up against the shore. I don't know how many I killed 'cause by that time they had floated away. I managed to pull myself up and skiffed away till I come up on a fisherman out working his boat. He saw me comin' from a distance and yelled to me.

"Did you kill anything?"

"I think I did," I answered.

"I think you did, too," he yelled when he saw me up closer.

You see, when that battery gun blew up it did it right in my face, knocking me out and ripping the skin off my face so that it was hangin' like a sheet off my chin. I must have been in shock 'cause I had no idea what I looked like. Now, neither one of us had a pocket knife, but we did have an old butter knife so he took it and sterilized it as good as he could over the stove lid and cut the rest of the skin off my chin. He didn't have no antiseptic or nothing like it on board, so he pulled some stuffing out of an old mattress down below and soaked it in the gas and oil from the boat engine, rubbing it all over my raw face and I'll tell you, I felt every bit of that.

The fisherman told me he'd carry me home if I'd go down below and rest, but I told him that I was waitin' for the next time and planned to shoot again. See, I still didn't know the kind of shape I was in, and I never did shoot again that day. I got home and lay in bed for two or three days till I could think straight, and I'll tell you, ten days later when that last scab was gone from my face, the only scar I had was this little mark above my eye and the six teeth I found in my skiff when I went to clean it out.

Leonard Ward

(At the right is Bill Smith.)

A BACHELOR and waterman his entire life, Leonard Ward was born in Crisfield, Maryland on October 4, 1913. Once an avid hunter, he gave it up when "it seemed like there were more wardens around than birds." Today he lives in Crisfield, still working on the bay and taking fishing parties in his spare time.

I HUNTED with a punt gun for about five years, I guess. I made it myself out of seamless tubin' and set it into my boat in a chock with a piece of rope lashed over the barrel to keep it from jumping up on me. Used it mostly for sneakin' up on geese out in the bars at night. The most I ever killed in one shot was fifteen; never did have one go off in my face, but a feller down in Lawsonia that I knew did. Had a battery [4 guns together] go off in his face and blinded him for some time. Left powder burns all around his eyes, too. That was one way you could tell who was usin' the big guns. My mother's cousin, who lived over on Smith Island, had one go off in his face, too, one night. Blinded him. Broke loose from the boat and ripped one side off. It was a damn cold night and there he was in this little skiff five or six miles offshore and couldn't see a damn thing. Luckily, it was real still and he could hear noises coming from the island so he leaned over to one side to keep the water from coming in and paddled that skiff back to the shore. He was damn lucky. 'Cause many of 'em never did come back when something like that happened.

It was about the only thing you could do around Crisfield to make money during the winter. You know, we was like the Indians, we had to make our livin' off what nature gave us and back then that was shootin' birds. We never really did get into shippin' them, 'cause we were so damn isolated here except for the railroad that would leave once a day. We just sold to the locals mainly and got by on that. I'd either go out by myself with a couple of friends or guiding a huntin' party. Back then, we shot mostly pintails, but you hardly see them around here anymore. Fact is, we got more damn wardens around here now than ducks it seems sometimes. Anyway, I used a roll-up blind that I'd take with me. That way you could go wherever the birds was, 'cause if you shot one spot one day they damn sure wasn't going to be there the next day. We'd set up on a bar mostly; put our stool out in the flats in front of us. My favorite spot was over on Smith Island—a place called Terrapin Sand, a bar about a mile long and some of the best shootin' any-where. It's all washed away now, though. Anyway, we'd never do any serious baitin' on these spots. Mostly if we baited, we did it for ourselves so the fowl would taste better.

I KNOW this feller who raised a Canada goose from the time it was a baby and used it for tolling. The goose's name was George, and all he'd have to do was walk outside his house and yell to him, "C'mon, George, we're going gunnin'," and that damn bird would follow him and jump right into the boat. Now, usually a tolling bird would have a wing clipped or be tied to a stake but not old George.

One time another friend of mine was out in South Marsh gunning when he saw a flock of geese start to pitch in sideways to a flock of decoys out of his range. They set in and old George came walking out of this blind, swam out to them, and strung them right into gunnin' range. Then he left the birds, swam ashore, and walked back into the blind. Well, nobody shot for a while and the birds just stayed out there swimming around the decoys. So this man snuck up on the blind and damned if the hunter wasn't asleep with old George sittin' right next to him watching the birds. Now, I've known this feller to be real truthful and I believe him. Myself, I've seen George sitting on a bar out near South Marsh with a flock of wild geese and that feller would call him and damned if George wouldn't leave and follow him. You could pick him out you know. He was a little brighter than a wild goose and moved differently. Yep, old George was one of the best tollers around Crisfield.

ME and Bill James, an old gunnin' buddy of mine, kept a blind down at Broad Creek right off the Manokin River that's still there today if you look on a chart.

We never used decoys when we shot there 'cause we always kept it baited. We'd put about one quart a day out, just enough to keep the birds coming round. Then, after about two weeks you'd know that they was ready to shoot. See, sometime you can see just a bit of oil on top of the water from corning them. Now, I know it comes off their feathers or droppings, and we'd always look for a sign of it to shoot. And, man, that fowl would be as yellow as a kernel of corn and just as good tasting.

I always shot a five-shot Browning automatic with twenty-eight-inch barrels. Never did fool with plugging guns when he was duckin'—bird hunting maybe, but not ducks. James had a Model 12 Winchester Pump, thirty-inch barrels that could hold seven shots. It was always unplugged too. Anyway we were sittin' out in this blind one morning early, with a good northwest breeze blowing when this flock of about twenty blackheads showed up, made a couple of passes over the blind, and started to come in. Well, I shot five times and got four, one crippled. James pumped his gun seven times and laid seven on their backs. When they land on their backs like that you know they're dead. He was the first person I ever saw or heard tell of that could do that. And then, just as I was about to shoot one cripple that I had down, I heard this bam! as his gun went off again, doing it for me. Not only had he shot seven birds with seven shots, but he'd reloaded and killed my cripple faster than I could. That son of a bitch could shoot that pump as fast as I could my automatic.

BILL JAMES had this fourteen-by-sixteen-foot gunning shack on some property he owned down near St. Pierre Island. It was a nice, tight little building, and if it got too cold, you could always go inside, light a fire, cook yourself a meal, and have a little nip. See, we always kept some local moonshine in there and usually a little food of some sort. Now, back then you could buy a gallon of this murky looking stuff which was pretty potent for three dollars or a gallon that was clear for five dollars and just as potent. We'd buy a gallon of each and mix 'em together. Hell, it made no difference if you got into them pretty good anyway. Now, this one time I got a deal on some sardines from a man around here. He was selling cases of them damn cheap, so I bought two for the shack. One was packed in mustard and one in oil in these little wooden boxes. He told me that there was twenty-four boxes to a case, but when I went to unload 'em it turned out there was fifty to a case! Now, that is a hell of a lot of sardines no matter how you look at it. We also kept the place pretty well stocked with ammo and sometimes a gun or two and on this day had at least five hundred shotgun shells, plus a real nice rifle of mine and a load of cartridges.

Now, before I get ahead of myself, let me tell you that Bill lent the shack to these two local boys for a couple of days to do some gunning. These boys were real characters and loved to get into the 'shine once in a while. They were doing real good down there, killing a mess of birds till this one day Peeler, which was the name of one of the boys, got cold and went inside to warm up. He left his buddy, King Cole, outside in the shore blind to shoot. Peeler stoked up the fire real good and got himself pretty well into the bootleg as he sat and looked out over the river. Sitting there, he saw these seven canvasbacks pitch into a nearby cove and drunk as he was decided he was going after them, so he picked up his shotgun and headed out after them. "Draggin' belly" he called it as he pulled himself across the ice and through the marsh till he just about got himself within range of them. Then they jumped up and flew off. Now that surprised the hell out of him 'cause Peeler could drag belly with the best of them. In a blind he wasn't much of a shot, but I'll bet he killed more black ducks by sneaking up on them than anybody around. Anyway, figuring something else must have spooked them, he sat up to take a look around and damned if he didn't see smoke billowing out of the shanty like crazy. Getting up, he ran just as fast as he could towards the shack to try and get the ammo and rifles out and just as he got up on her, he could see the flames starting to leap out of the door. He swung it open anyway and just as he did, heard the most god-awful noise through all that smoke. Then all hell broke loose as the sardines, which were in wooden boxes and soaked in oil, started going off like little rockets, shootin' all over the damn place. He hit the ground and got out as fast as he could and him and King Cole sat and watched the place burn to the ground with the ammo going off and those rifles inside. He said it didn't take long, no more than a couple of minutes and the whole place fell in and that was the end of that old place.

I DIDN'T pay much attention to the airplanes the wardens used at first, but James was scared to death of them. He'd lie right down in the blind if one came near 'cause they could take your damn picture from up there, you know. If we'd see them coming in time, we'd jump right into the skiff and head away so that when they flew over all they'd see was an empty blind. But when they started using a seaplane, that was a different story. That's when we stopped using our offshore blinds and moved in to the concrete ones. This one night, me and James was out baitin' and shootin' and on our way back in, James thought he saw what looked like a light go on and off from the shore. But I didn't pay much attention to it at first. I was feelin' pretty good, you know, and we both had us a sack full of ducks still in our legal limit that we shot over bait that night. Now, I don't know if you know it or not, but a duck can't swallow corn or nothing under water. That's why when he comes up sometimes you'll see him with a real thick spot in his neck that's full of corn. He'll swallow it, then dive again for more. So if you shoot him soon as he pops up, you'll most likely find corn in him if he's over bait. Anyway, as we were comin' home up the river that night we shot this crippled dipper, picked it up, and threw it up forward behind the gas tank. James wanted me to hide it in my waders but I told him no. We got back to James's property, loaded the ducks and decoys into the old Plymouth we had, and started off, and just as soon as we were off James's land, this federal game warden stops us. He walked up to the car and over to James's side and asked us if we'd had any luck.

"Yeah, we shot our limit," I told him.

"If you don't mind, I'd like to have a look at them to see what kind of condition they're in," he said.

Well, you've got to remember that we'd shot them over bait, and I was getting a little nervous that he might find some corn in their throats. We both had a bagful and as I dumped mine out in front of the headlights, damned if three or four kernels of corn didn't fall right on top of them. I just about shit

141

myself, but I don't know whether he saw them or not 'cause he just reached down and picked up every bird in my pile and in James's and felt right down their necks to see if there was something in them. He did every damn duck that way, and I know some of them was still full of corn 'cause we shot them just as they popped up like I told you before. He didn't say a damn word about it, and just asked us if our guns was plugged and if we had our licenses or not. Then he thanked us, got into his car, and, now, you figure it out! But I'll tell you, I'm glad that we forgot that little crippled dipper we shot 'cause then he'd a had us for sure. Maybe not though.

THAT same warden that stopped me and Bill James caught Bill once. He had a brother named Tom who was quite a character. He could drink like hell and never held the same job for very long, but he managed to get himself all around the world and had some stories to tell about it, too. This one particular time he'd been up in Canada managing a mink farm and learning taxidermy from some fellow. It turned out he had a good knack for mountin' animals, too, but not so much for raisin' mink 'cause he got fired. He came back down here after a while and was staying with Bill. Once in a while we'd take him out to shoot some birds so he could mount them. This one particular time I wasn't with them, but this is what happened:

It was a Saturday when they set out in Bill's speedboat. That old boat would do forty miles an hour back then which was really something. Anyway, Bill had a stamp and license so he was legal, but his brother never did bother to get one, but

brought a gun anyway. They just never gave no thought to running into a warden at that time. They headed off towards a spot near St. Pierre Island to rig out, looking for flocks sittin' on the water on the way down. See, you could circle the flocks with the boat and the healthy ducks would jump off and fly away while the cripples would dive. Then you'd wait for the cripples and shoot them. It was doing them a favor, puttin' 'em out of their misery, and they made the best mounts usually 'cause they had very little fat on them. They got down near St. Pierre Island and set out about sixty Ward brothers decoys that we'd paid a dollar fifty a piece for, hid the boat in some grass on the shoreline, and sat in it waitin'. They must have been in a line of flight, 'cause in no time at all they'd knocked down five of those ruddy ducks. "Sleepy heads," we call them, and one blackhead. Old Bill was a smart man and never missed much out on the water. He was always lookin'. You know, scannin' the area to see what was going on around him. And this day was no different.

Right after they shot their last duck he saw this boat about one hundred yards off in the distance, tonging. "That don't look right," he said to Tom. "Who'd be out here tonging on a Saturday? I don't like the way that looks one bit."

So they stopped shootin' and kept watching the boat. Gradually, it moved a little closer and closer. Finally Bill said to his brother, "Give me that gun of yours and lay down flat in the boat." Down they both went and James crawled over the side with the gun into the river on his hands and knees. He started to bury it in the sand. Then he got back into the boat and lay there listening for a bit. He finally whispered, "Okay, let's go," to Tom, and up they both stood.

Well, you can imagine how surprised they were when they stood up and not twenty-five feet away was two wardens standing in the tonging boat, watchin' them. One of them was the federal man, about six foot six, who'd broken up a duck trappin' ring on Smith Island. I always liked the guy, even

144

though he laid for me and Bill for three days and nights once. Anyway, they asked Bill and his brother what they was up to and they told them they was just out trying to get themselves something to eat, some clams, crabs, and ducks. This guy wasn't buying that line, and he got out of his boat into about three feet of water and started thrashing around the bottom, but never close enough to where Bill had hid the gun. Now, the river was moving pretty good, and that gun was in shallow water, but it never came uncovered. Finally, the warden got back into his boat which was alongside Bill now and seeing only one gun, said, "It's funny, you two only come out here with one gun." He reached over and picked up Bill's gun, pumped her seven times and out came seven shells. He had no plug in her. "Well," he said, "I'm gonna have to confiscate her and give you a summons for having no plug."

"Hell," Bill said, relieved to just get away with that, "you can't take her. We still want to do some gunnin'."

"I can't help that," the warden said. "Law's the law. You can pick it up Monday morning, first thing when you come up to pay the fine."

And that's what he did. It cost him the maximum back then, $25.50, and you know, now that I think of it, I never did find out if they got the buried gun back.

HAVE you ever shot a 22 Swift? Man, that is some kind of gun. One day I was down at Fishing Island with Bill James, and we had one with us. James saw this lone water witch [merganser] out there about fifty yards offshore in flat calm water, swimmin' back and forth.

"I'm gonna try him," James said.

"Shit," I said, "why don't you leave that poor old water witch alone."

Well, it finally bothered him enough so that he went and got the gun out of the car, put a couple of shells in it, and laid that barrel right over the front of the hood so he had that old bird sighted in. You know, when he pulled that trigger there wasn't a damn splash at all in that water, no feathers flew—nothing! But that old water witch came apart right in two, and the pieces sank about a foot and a half apart, so help me God. Cut him right half in two! It looked like magic to me—and not a damn splash of water or nothing! I know one thing—he didn't feel nothing.

146

By the way, this is what finally happened to my gunning partner, Tom. He'd been going out with this real goodlookin' young girl for a while and was supposed to get married to her. But when it came time for the wedding, Tom shocked the hell out of all of us and married the girl's mother instead. It didn't last very long. They was always at each other like cats and dogs and finally got into this big row one night in the kitchen. To this day, nobody's really sure what happened, but Tom left with one hand all sliced up. Now, she says she was protecting herself, and he says she stabbed him, so who knows. Anyway, shortly after that he took off for Canada and got himself a job on that mink ranch that I told you about earlier. I guess he was doing pretty good, too, learning taxidermy and all. Then, after about six months, one night he got all fired up and decided he was gonna tell the owner how to run the place. Needless to say, that didn't go over at all and that was the end of that job. He must have got himself back home as far as Baltimore 'cause on the twenty-third of December that year, his father got a telegram from him that cost two dollars and fifty cents.

It said, "I'm a victim of circumstance and need twenty-five dollars."

Well, after not seeing his son for a year or so he didn't hesitate to send the money. Besides, he was glad to have him coming home in time for Christmas. Well, Christmas came and went and with no sign of Tom. Then, about a month or so later his dad gets another telegram. This one costs him twenty-five dollars, came from the police department in Cairo, Egypt, and said again: "I'm a victim of circumstance and need twenty-five hundred dollars."

His father said the hell with him and never sent the money. But, somehow Tom managed to get himself home and whenever anybody'd ask him about it, he'd just say that he'd gotten on the wrong train!

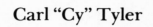
Carl "Cy" Tyler

CARL "CY" TYLER was born in the "Neck District" of Crisfield, Maryland, on September 4, 1917, moving when he was small to Tangier Island to live for a while with his mother's family.

Crabbing in the summer and trapping and hunting in the winter is how he describes his childhood, a way of life that has continued for him to the present day.

He still lives in the Neck District with his family and when not there can be found at a local seafood store sitting on the "liar's bench" with a bunch of his friends, swapping stories.

THERE'S a man over on Tangier Island named Ray Crockett. Now, he could tell you some stories. Years back, he kept a couple of houseboats out on Watts Island during the gunning season. They'd pull the houseboats out during a real high tide and leave them right off in one of the coves on high ground, lived there right through the season, taking people out gunning, and when there was nobody to go, they'd gun themselves. It was quite a place back then. See, corning was still legal, and they kept a whole building full of it. Each night they'd bait the blinds, and next day there'd be no problem killing birds.

Ray always said it was the best place he ever hunted. And some variety of ducks, too. Every kind you can imagine and loads of geese.

He never used a punt gun. Never had to. Had enough to shoot as it was. And, remember, the limits were much bigger then and the weather was cold in the winter, not like it is today—mild right through January.

I USED to hunt quite a bit with Lem and Steve Ward, the famous decoy carvers. Hunted with Lem for about eight years steady and a little bit with Steve. This was way back when they were just starting to fool around with carving decoys. Steve used to use a big gun like his dad. Not many know it but his dad was a big market hunter and duck trapper around these parts, and for a while Steve followed right after him. That man Ray Crockett that I just told you about told me a funny story about Steve once. Seems he was going gunning one night out near Tangier Island with his big gun and stopped at Ray Crockett's store to buy some shotgun shells for shooting the cripples that you usually had after the big gun went off. Now, around here, we talk funny enough, I guess, but out on Tangier they got a language all their own, you know. So, anyway, he walked into Ray's store asking for some "hells." "What'ya mean 'hells,'" they teased him like they didn't know what he was talking about.

"Hells, man, I wanta buy some 'hells.'"

They went back and forth for a while till Steve started getting real mad. Then they pulled out a box of shells for him. And they all had a good laugh over it.

Now Lem never did use a big gun that I know of, but like I told you, him and me did quite a bit of gunning together at one time. He was older than me but I had a real good spot that I gunned and I'd take him with me usually.

In fact, the day my boy was born, thirty years ago this past November 12th, the first day of gunning season, me and Lem was upstreet waiting for the tide to change so we could go out. They come by and told me my wife was at the hospital with a big bouncing baby boy.

"You should hurry up and get down there to see him," they said.

"Hell, he'll be there when I get back," I told them, and off me and Lem went gunning.

We were after baldpates and pintails that day, and we didn't have the fancy calls to call them like they use today. We used a damn police whistle to call 'em. It worked real well, too. We just kept trying and trying them till we got them to work just right. Then, man, you could get those birds to come in like nothing. Other times we'd just walk through the marshes round Cedar Island and jump up ducks. Hardly ever use a dog, though. Too much trouble out in the marsh.

The wardens chased us plenty, too, don't think they didn't. They never did catch me, though, till last year. They lay in the marshes for four days waiting to catch me and they finally did, just 'cause I wasn't using my head. I knew they were there then, too, just didn't pay them no mind. When they finally did catch me, they made it a federal not a state offense. I guess 'cause they'd been trying so hard for so long to catch me. They gave me a fine and took my migratory bird license away for a year. I think that's it though. I don't believe I'll shoot a duck again. They've just taken all the fun out of it.

Thomas Reed

EARLY in the nineteeth century Joshua Reed, a seafaring man from Maine, was shipwrecked off Chincoteague Island during a violent storm. He managed to get ashore and decided to settle on the island. Joshua Reed was the grandfather of Thomas Reed who was born on Chincoteague May 24, 1901.

Thomas Reed grew up in an era when market hunting was an honorable profession, passed down from fathers and grandfathers. There were no game laws, and the "season" was set by nature. But when the law finally made market hunting illegal in the early 1930s, Tom changed from shooting ducks to raising them. He even ran a wild duck farm for tourists on Chincoteague and later in Florida until a hurricane in 1933 destroyed most of his property there. Returning to Chincoteague, Tom turned to fishing, clamming, crabbing, and gunning for a living until the tightening of game laws and especially the advent of the seaplane switched the advantage definitely to the side of the law. One of the last market hunters to give it up, Tom finally hung up his tools and started to adapt to the changing times.

Word of his vast knowledge of the marshes and bays became known, and Tom was hired by Walter Reed Army Medical Center to run their scientific research programs on Chincoteague. Catching insects, fowl, and mammals for medical studies, Tom quickly became an invaluable asset to the program, and has served it to this day.

He lives with Marjorie, his wife of many years, at Deep Creek where he can be found gazing out over the bays, writing poetry, or helping out in the family seafood business when time allows.

I STARTED trappin' and huntin' ducks when I was about ten years old. You see, everybody that grew up on these coastal islands made their livin' out of the mud and the marshes harvesting these crops from the sea. Like crabs, oysters, fishing in the warmer times, and huntin' in the winter. We were taught by our fathers or older brothers how to do these things. You didn't learn nothing like this out of no books. You had to grow up with it.

When I started doin' it there was no game laws—everything was legal. We'd sell to a local buyer or ship them up to a market, but mostly the local buyer would take everything you could kill.

I was seventeen before I ever heard of a game law or a game warden, but by that time my life had already been set. It was my way of life. I didn't know anything else. We got along pretty good when the laws first started. 'Course the legal limit was pretty high. Then they started to cut it down year after year till it was down to around ten, then all of us who depended on it had to figure out a way quick to get around the law. 'Course a lot of them ended up getting caught, but I never did. And I kept it up longer than anybody else. I had a rig of twenty Ira Hudson balsa wood goose stools that I still own today and the middles of them was all hollowed out so I could put a bird in each one of them. Now, twenty of them that way, and my legal ten, and I didn't have such a bad day. I kept that up till I was hired by the government on this medical research program. Then they was paying me a good legal livin' wage.

W E started being outlaws here as soon as the game laws came into being. I always compared us to foxes or eagles. A fox don't know it's bad to raid a chicken coop, and an eagle doesn't think he's doing anything wrong when he swoops down and takes a baby lamb out of a pasture. They're just doing what comes naturally—tryin' to get something to eat and that's the way we were. Oh, at first it wasn't bad 'cause the daily limit was thirty-five so you could still make a livin' doin' it. Then later on, they cut it down to twenty-five which still wasn't too bad, 'cause you couldn't always get that many every day, but then a year or two later they cut it down to ten, and I couldn't make no living on ten ducks a day. I had a family started then, and I needed those ducks to sell. Well, right about that time I found an old balsa wood life raft on the beach and I took it over to Ira Hudson who now is a famous decoy carver.

"Ira," I told him, "I want you to make me twenty geese decoys out of this balsa wood."

"Tom, you can't make good decoys out of that balsa wood. It beats up too easy and won't hold paint."

I told him I had a small skiff and I needed some light decoys. I didn't tell him what I really had in mind.

He made the decoys for me, finally, and I took 'em home and hollowed the bottoms out. Now I could hide twenty birds in them and with my ten legal ones it made up a good huntin' day, and I didn't have to worry about gettin' caught. That's what I thought at the time anyway. Years later I was out gunnin' in the marshes one mornin' and had done real good, had all the decoys filled up and some in the boat. I saw this little airplane comin' with pontoons on it. Never had seen one before like it. He saw me and swooped right over top of me and landed in a creek not far away. Now, I'm standin' there next to my boat watching this and out jumps a man and a Chesapeake Bay retriever who starts runnin' through the marsh sniffing. The man came over to me and explained that he was a warden and the dog had been trained to sniff out ducks that had been hidden in the marshes. Well, I felt pretty nervous now with this damn warden standing right next to me so I started thinking real hard and real fast.

"Is he a pretty good retriever?" I asked.

"The best there is."

"Mind if I try him out?" I said.

"Go right ahead."

So I picked up one of my "legal" ducks and I threw it just as hard as I could in the opposite direction. The dog jumped in the water, swam after it as pretty as could be, picked it up, and brought it back to the warden. But it didn't satisfy the damn dog. He went right for the decoys again.

"Mind if I do it again? That was pretty," I said.

"No, go ahead. It's good training for my dog."

I threw ducks for that dog till he was about wore out, and I never did use my decoys again as long as that warden was around with his dog.

YEARS ago we would go "down the bay" in these bay boats about thirty foot long, [sleeping] up to seven people. They were usually run by an older man from the island [Chincoteague] and each person who went down the bay would bring a smaller boat that would be towed down to hunt, fish, and clam in. We'd go sometimes for two weeks at a time, 'specially in the winter when we went to hunt. We'd hunt for a week and take the birds to Willis Wharf to sell, then go back out and hunt for another week and bring those birds home to sell and eat. We always had bread, meat, and molasses aboard, which was our basic diet, and we'd add whatever we was catching or shootin' to that. Now, in the summertime when those laughing gulls was nesting we'd stop and take a bushel basket of eggs, sometimes, to fry up.

On one of these trips me and my cousin, Corbin Reed, took one of those headlights off the big boat and set out in our smaller boat to light ducks. It was a real pretty night, calm, and flat water. We killed a few ducks, then all of a sudden, with no warning, the wind come out of the north and started blowin' a gale, tide risin', the whole time. We started off right away in our little boat through this storm tryin' to find the big boat, but we had the only light so there was no way we could spot it from a distance in the dark with this storm blowing. Meanwhile, it's blowin' harder and harder all the time with the tides still rising, and now we've got waves breakin' over the boat so I paddled like hell and Corb bailed the water. We finally made it about five miles to a place called The Draft. Now, right near there we knew an old man lived alone out in the marsh called Frank Marsh, so we took off lookin' for him. About midnight, covered with mud from wadin' through the marsh and soakin' wet from crossing guts and creeks, we finally came up on his house, knocked on the door, and saw a light come on. He opened the door holdin' his musket. 'Course he didn't know who the hell we was standin' there lookin' like hell in the middle of this gale holdin' two automatics. We told him our

161

story and he took us in and made some coffee. He kept us
there till daylight, lettin' us dry out, and talkin'. Then we all
went back out into the marsh to find our small boat. We give
him all the ducks we'd shot and by now, with the sun up and
the storm over, we could see the big boat off in the distance.
We thanked Frank and paddled back to the boat, and I'll tell
you they were some damn surprised to see us comin'. 'Course
they'd given us up for drowned. Could you blame 'em?

You remember those twenty hollowed out decoys I was tellin' you about before? The ones I'd carry with me gunnin' and hide the ducks inside? Well, one day I'd been out gunnin' and shot twenty-eight black duck. Now, by this point the government had lowered our limit to ten a day but I had my twenty hidden and as I came ashore that morning I also had a warden waitin' there for me. He popped out of the bushes, walked up to my skiff, and looked inside.

"Gee, Tom, looks like you didn't hit 'em that good this mornin'," he said.

"Well, they can't all be good mornings," I said, stuffing my decoys into a potato sack as fast as I could. "Least I won't starve this week," and I jumped out of my skiff with my decoy sack over my back and headed off to home, smiling to myself.

163

WE used to shoot loads of shorebirds. People who weren't raised here for the most part don't know what a yellowleg or curlew is. But when I first started hunting, we shot them all the time, and it was legal then.

If company was coming for dinner, we'd go out on a flat and kill a basketful and take a load of soft crabs, too, at the same time. They were both all over the place then. Later on, when they made the law against shootin' them we still did it 'cause we loved to eat 'em.

But then we'd carry a sack with a big rock in it, and if the warden started comin' after us, we'd just throw that sack of birds overboard and let it sink right to the bottom. That worked fine as long as the warden didn't see you throw it overboard 'cause then he might scrape it up. So what I'd do was, when I got finished fillin' up a sackful, I'd tie the top with a cord that was attached to the bottom of the boat. Then, re-gardless whether he saw me throw it overboard or not he could scrape all day long and not find the sack 'cause it was right under me and wherever I went, it went with me.

I was out oystering one evening right off the refuge [Assateague] when I saw these geese pitch in so I figured I'd wait till it got dark, then go in and light them with this flashlight I had with me. Well, I was walkin' up on them when John Buckalew jumped out of the bushes and yelled, "Tom Reed, you're on a refuge with a gun."

I said, "I ain't done nothin'. I just came here to see who you were."

He grabbed for the gun, and we wrestled back and forth for a while till it slipped free of both of us and fell into the marsh mud. He jumped after it, and I grabbed him right around his waist. I was damned if I was goin' to let him get my gun, and we both went down into the mud. Now, I don't know when he hit me, but when I came to I was laying there with blood running down my arm.

He said, "Let's talk this thing over."

"There ain't nothing to talk about," I said. "You had no business hittin' me. I wasn't trying to hurt you."

He turned and started off. I picked up my gun and was just about to blow the top of his head off when I realized he'd married a Chincoteague girl, and I couldn't do that to her. Walter Clark did end up shooting him later, though.

GOOD LORD, man, I've been chased just about all my life by wardens till I gave it up. I've got a son who's sixty now that used to trap with me. We go out the bay and into the marshes and set out traps. They knew I was doin' it, and they wanted to catch me real bad, too. This one Saturday mornin' before daylight, I went down with my brother-in-law, took my little boat, went down the bay, emptied my duck traps, and started home. The wind started blowin' hard and I had water comin' in the boat from the waves lappin' up on the sides. Now, in twenty years, I'd never landed in any spot but my own landing, but this day I said to my brother-in-law, we called him Bird.

I said, "Bird, let's stop along shore and walk home. I'm too cold and wet to stay out here." So we stopped. Went into the bushes with our bags of ducks, wrung their necks to kill them all, put 'em back in the bags, and started home.

We got home and took the ducks down into the basement where we laid them out on the floor to keep real cool. Then we went upstairs where I cooked breakfast for Bird, my wife, son, and myself. Now, generally on a Saturday morning, my son would go clammin'. So, after breakfast he started off down this path to the bay, and damned if I didn't see him comin' back shortly after.

He came back inside and said, "Dad, there's three men laying out there in the bushes, and I don't know who they are."

"Well, I'd better go see what's going on," I said and started off towards my mother's yard and I could see them now, walking down the road. So I jumped in my old Essex automobile and picked them up while they was walkin'. I told them I was headed into town and asked them what they was doin' up here so early in the mornin'.

"We heard of some violatin' goin' on up in this area, and we're checkin' on it."

'Course they didn't know who I was. Darn fools!

167

WE had lots of different ways of lightin' ducks. If you had the moon with you, it was usually bright enough that you could see the flocks, but dark nights you had to get what we called a "daylight shot." That's when the sun is just goin' down or an "early morning shot" when the light is comin' out of the east. You'd get yourself behind the ducks and let that early light show you where they was.

This one morning I was out trying to get myself an early morning shot, and I came up on this flock, shot into them, and killed eight. And, right away I heard this motor start up, but I didn't think nothin' of it. Just thought it was one of the boys takin' out a huntin' party. So I kept goin' down moon, tryin' to get up on another flock of birds before it got too light. Now, as I'm movin' down the marsh, I happened to glance to my west and saw this little boat comin' towards me. Right away I knew exactly what was happening now, 'cause I could see the silhouette of a man I knew to be my wife's cousin, and a warden to boot! So I took off rowing through the marsh as fast as I could in that little skiff. Pulled it across a big moss bar and kept goin'. Now, when that warden got to the bar, his boat was too big for him to drag across, so he had to turn back and find a way through the marsh to come after me. Meanwhile, I was ashore and had taken some of the marsh mud and had rubbed it all over my clothes, face, arms, and legs hopin' even if he did spot me, he wouldn't recognize me. Then I took off rowin' again. Now, I was pretty young and strong, and I kept going till I got to what we call Oyster Bay which is full of "oyster rocks" and, again, I could get around them, but there was no way that warden's dory with an outboard was goin' to follow me, so he gave it up. I come on home, hid my ducks, and cleaned up, and that warden never did come around my place lookin' for me. 'Course he probably thought we would have shot him, and maybe he was right about that.

168

DID you ever hear tell of Owen Steele? He used to be a federal game warden out of Cambridge, Maryland. He was Jim Williams's and John Buckalew's boss. I had some muskrat traps out here, right straight across from my house and one morning early I went out to fish [empty] my traps, and I saw three people in a pole boat pushin' around till they got to shore and landed. I didn't give them much thought at the time. I guessed they were probably rabbit hunters or something like that. So I went along fishing my traps, come on home, forgot all about them. That afternoon I went back out to bait my duck traps with my wife's brother, Bird. We had the traps open so the ducks could go in and feed, then get back out again. We'd do that for a few days, then close up the funnel once we had them comin' in good. The first trap hadn't been discovered yet 'cause there was still corn in it, so we went up to the next one, threw some corn in it, and all of a sudden I see these three guys comin' towards us, holdin' shotguns and what looked like a rifle.

Now they was comin' at us pretty fast so I told Bird, "Bird, we better get out of here," which we did, and the bastards started shootin' at us. They got so close that mud was splattering up on our coats from the bullets landing. We run as hard as we could run, got into the boat, got away from them, but they still kept shootin' at us. Luckily, they were poor shots. We got back home as fast as we could, and I changed into my good clothes right away. Went into town and stopped at the post office first to get my mail. Well, the postman asked where I was goin', all dressed up, and I told him I was on my way to Pocomoke. Then I went in the hardware store and told them the same thing, tryin' to establish myself an alibi. I guess three or four months went by, and one day this Owen Steele stopped by my house, knocked on my door, and asked me to come outside and talk for a few minutes. I was just gettin' ready to go out and bait my traps but I figured I'd better see what he had on his mind.

He says, "Tom, I've got a letter here from Washington, and they've got some questions that they want to ask you about your permit to raise live ducks. You've got to be there by nine tomorrow morning."

I said, "I can't go to Washington. I ain't got no money to get there."

He said, "Well, I'll take you up as far as Cambridge tonight."

"That don't matter to me," I said, "I still ain't got no money to get there."

Now I thought he might be playing some sort of trick on me so I told him to give me a couple of hours to see if I couldn't round up some money.

"I've got to go down to the telephone office and call Washington to tell them if you're coming," he said.

So I told him to go ahead, that I'd try to make it. Now, right after he left I took off and went into town, stopped at the telephone office, and asked the girls there if Steele had been in to make a phone call.

"We can't give you any information," they said. "It's against the rules."

"Well," I said, "if he hadn't been here, you could tell me that, couldn't you?"

"Yeah, I guess we could," they said.

"That's all I want to know," I said.

I took off home. I borrowed fifty dollars from my brother-in-law. Steele carried me to Cambridge and put me in a boarding house for the night. Next mornin' they was going to pick me up early and take me to Washington. That night I lay in bed thinking of all the questions they could ask me and what I'd tell them. I never slept a wink. Steele picked me up next morning and carried me up there. When I got there, they had nine people who questioned me for two solid hours, not about my permit to raise birds but about some damn guy they wanted to get for shippin' birds. And he wasn't from Chincoteague. I told them I didn't know nothing about what they was asking me, so after the two hours we took a break to get something to eat. This one man took me out to get something to eat, and he was acting real friendly towards me. Like he was on my side, you know.

"Between me and you, Tom," he said, "don't you really know a lot more than you're talking about?"

"No," I said. "I don't know nothing about no ducks being shipped."

Well, he come back with a stack of papers and said, "Tom, we've got enough evidence here to put you away for six years if you don't cooperate with us."

They must have thought they was dealing with some sort of idiot, but I knew what they was up to. Heck, I've seen stuff like that in the movies even. Anyway, I didn't tell them anything and coming back to Cambridge, Steele tried the same thing.

"This thing ain't over yet, you know, Tom. You'll still have to go to court."

"If I have to go, I will," I told him, "but I still don't know nothing about no duck shippin'."

Well, a couple of weeks later I come home and found this notice tacked on my door that I had to appear in federal court down in Norfolk for attemptin' to capture wild ducks. That night I sat down and wrote a letter to the judge in Norfolk. His name was Luther D. Way. I'll never forget that. I told him that for people livin' out here on these islands it was damn hard to make a livin' back then and sometimes we had to sidestep the law, and couldn't I just pay the smallest fine possible and not have to travel all the way down to Norfolk? Well, he never answered me, so I had to go down there and borrow money to hire a lawyer. Now, this lawyer had gone to school with the prosecuting attorney and he told me he'd talk to him and see what he could do. He came back and told me that I'd have to appear in court but if I plead guilty he could get me off with a small fine. I told him, "If I've got to travel all the way down here I'm not pleadin' guilty. I'm gonna fight this damn thing." Now, Steele had sworn that he could identify me by the cap and boots I was wearin'. Now you know as well as I do that he said that 'cause he saw me wearin' them the day he come over to my house to take me to Washington. And the other thing he done was to go up to Pocomoke the day I'd said I had and ask around a bunch of shopkeepers if they'd seen me up there shoppin'. So he'd subpoenaed some of them to appear in court. Now, my wife had been to Pocomoke that day and bought some stuff so I had those slips with me. Now the prosecuting attorney said, "All that proves is that your wife went shopping that day," which was true, but one shopkeeper testified that he never saw her shopping without me which helped me out quite a bit. When the judge asked me about it and why my wife's name was on all the slips I told him that most times we went shopping I never bought anything. I just went to tote all the bundles. Well, he smiled when he heard that, so I figured he was on my side a bit.

172

Now, because of some discrepancies by the officers and a lot of luck on my side, the judge threw it out, but he told me it was real close. Then, again in front of the same judge on the same charge, Jim Williams had set me up this time, and he and another warden had got together and worked out a story that they were holdin' to. Their stories were so much alike that everybody knew they made them up. So the judge threw out the charges again. And that was the last time I had to go down there.

Paul Marshall

P AUL M ARSHALL was born October 6, 1914 at Long-
branch, at that time a settlement near Tylerton, Smith Island,
Maryland.

He spent his years oystering, crabbing, duck trapping,
hunting, evading the wardens, and serving as a guide for
Glenn L. Martin, the Baltimore aircraft builder.

Later in his life, he took to decoy carving and was recognized as one of the best in the country until recently, when ill
health forced him to give it up.

A truly talented and outspoken man, he lives today in
Tylerton and can be found either at home or at Marshall's
store swapping gunning stories and talking politics.

I DON'T know if there's anybody in their time who's had more gunning than I did. And I'd still be out there if I could. Now, my father, when he got sick, he acted like he didn't want to go anymore, but I have as much desire to go now as I ever did. It nearly kills me to have to stay here and not be able to go gunning. Don't get me wrong, though, I have no complaints. But I still have that desire to go.

The way you see the harbor out there now, all nice and open water, well, in the winter that'd be all frozen over and when it was frozen hard enough, we'd walk from Tylerton down to Horse Hammock Point, towing a sled. That was always a good gunnin' spot 'cause when everything else'd be frozen the tide would come up and with the wind reeling out of the northwest it would push the ice out and open up the water so birds would always be laying in there like you wouldn't believe. You could shoot twenty-five birds and get ten different species, but it was always bitter cold down there.

Now, if we couldn't get down to the Point, we might get into one of those old crab houses with an air hole around it and sit there all day shootin' birds.

I'd say we had some of the best waterfowl shootin' on the East Coast here until the government moved in and took over the marshes on the Maryland side. Now, on the Virginia side, the Chesapeake Bay Foundation owns all the marsh and they're the nicest bunch of people you'd ever want to meet. They'd never bother you, but the government—Christ, they're a damn public nuisance. They're not just satisfied havin' their laws. They've got to take over the land so you've really got to do what they say. There just ain't no excuse for it on a place this small.

I'LL tell you, I've been run down by government 'copters, boats, and every damn thing in the world. We been chased and shot at for over one hundred years out here, trying to make a living. Yeah, they got me more than several times and once in a while they was even right, but a couple of times it didn't happen that way.

One day, my brother and me was out, and they come up to us. We didn't have nothing on us, but we weren't takin' no lip from them either so the bastard put an assault charge on me. Now, I'm assaultin' you right now as much as I did him. So, after three or four months of going back and forth to Baltimore to court, my damn lawyer advised me to plead guilty and throw myself on the mercy of the court. It cost me three hundred dollars for this smart ass to come up with that. So I did it, hoping to get let off, but they put a seven hundred and fifty dollar fine on me instead. I even had people come up to me afterwards and tell me I should appeal, but, hell, I didn't want to go through that again.

One other time we was out here about three or four hundred yards off my dock, gettin' ready to load up on ducks when this helicopter from the Department of Natural Resources starts comin' right at us. They ain't satisfied leaving it up to one agency, they've got to bring everybody in on it. So, here they come after us. Well, my boy was with us so I put him ashore right away. He took off, hid his gun under the house, and ran down to the church where he hid in the steeple. We shoved off in the meantime just as the 'copter was landing. So they took off again after us. I knew the bastards would damn near cut our heads off with that thing so I held up an oar, swinging it around to keep them off us. We landed the boat again and took off towards the store where a pretty good-sized crowd had formed by this time, and we mixed right in with them. Now, by this time, they'd landed again and here comes the damn fools down to the store wantin' to know if they could borrow a skiff 'cause they'd dropped something in the creek—

probably a damn camera. I told him no.

"Nobody ain't gonna let you have nothin' to get nothin' and if you don't get out of here we going to bury you."

He took off pretty fast then and left, but the same son of a gun got me again, put two charges on me, and got me convicted on both. I appealed one of them, but they found me guilty just the same. Then about a week later they sent my money back in the mail. Now, do you think they thought I was guilty?!

WHEN I was a boy, I'd go out gunning with my Dad or we'd take out parties. Some of those people just couldn't believe how many birds we had around here without baiting 'em. The most ducks and geese I ever killed at once was without bait. There used to be so many birds out here you just wouldn't believe it. Now, here is what a lot of people don't understand. You might be out here hunting and not see a bird if the tide's up, but if it's the right kind of day and the tide starts to fall, they're going to start coming around that feedin' bar. 'Course, on a real rough day you might get geese and ducks anywhere. But I've killed geese and ducks and seen them fly for hours and hours.

I've seen some of the best gunning around here and I think if the government hadn't come in and started to mess with this place, we'd still have it. But they think they know it all. 'Course all you've got to do is look around this place and you can see they don't.

I'VE never known anyone to get killed or hurt with a punt gun, but I will tell you a close call somebody had. This feller was shovin' around before daybreak with his gun up in the Holland Strait when he heard a goose callin'. He shooed over towards where he could hear the goose and came up on this big flock. So he lay down in the skiff, paddled in with his hand paddles, lined her up, and set her off, and, Christ, he got the biggest damn surprise of his life. Right in the middle of the flock was a man who luckily was squatted down in his sink box callin'. The damn flock turned out to be a spread of decoys and a couple of tollin' geese. Well, that man raised up out of that box like a bat out of hell, yellin', "Who in the hell are you and

what kind of damn thing is that, anyway?" Scared him half to death. Must have been a city man from one of the clubs down there. Well, the feller turned his skiff around and poled out of there like you wouldn't believe.

IF you were to bring my grandfather back today and tell him he couldn't use the big gun anymore, he'd say, "Carry me back," 'cause that was his life. That's all he did when the birds was around. What money he made back then was from gunnin'. In his day, I would say there were twenty of the big guns here. Now, there're only two and 'course they don't get used. Not that anybody's sayin' anyway. Sometimes, back then, three or four skiffs might go out together and as a boy I'd wait outside just to hear them go off. Windows would shake in houses here at times. Yeah, that was really something.

Hell, the young people today aren't even interested in doin' it. There's nothing stoppin' them from doing geese at night. They're just not interested. Anyway, Bill DuPont sent his man through here a while ago and bought up all the guns that was still around and available and the Warden Hildebrand carried five off himself. He was something—posed as a taxidermist here for a while over at Rhodes Point, then came down on a bunch of the boys. Now, nobody went to jail, but those guns was the price they paid for it. Never was any record of his raid here.

Yep, them wardens was something. I knew a couple of fellers here years ago who was out catching oysters, so one night for dinner they shot themselves a couple of ducks to eat out of season and damned if the warden didn't come along, sneak up on them and took the ducks right out of the pot they was cookin' in. Yup, a great bunch of fellers they were.

My grandfather told me the most birds he ever killed with one shot from the punt gun was twelve geese. Like I was tellin' you before, there's no way that you could kill thousands in one night. Another feller I know got sixty-seven pintail in one shot and another bunch killed one hundred and eight brant in one shot. But that's one time, they never did it again. Christ, we had so many brant here then, if they'd stay'd still for you, you could've walked to Crisfield on 'em.

Now, when everybody was done gunnin', they'd bring their birds down to my dad's store to pick 'em and before I went gunnin' when I was still real young, I'd wait for 'em to come in. I'd grab myself a bunch of geese and all the ducks I could, get paid ten cents for a goose and the same for a pair of ducks. Sometimes four or five of us would pick eighty or ninety birds. I've seen my mother and another woman pick two tubfuls in one day.

Now, all the feathers flying around the store would raise hell with all the bulk goods they carried, get into the bales of goods and mix up with it so they had to stop cording it that way. Hell, the birds had to be picked somewhere and it was as good a place as any.

We'd pick every damn feather off those birds and use what we needed for pillows and mattresses. Everybody had down beds then. It took about fifty pounds to make a mattress and two pillows and, man, that's a lot of feathers. What was left over went to a feller who used to fill bags full to twenty pounds each, put five of them into an old flour sack, and ship them to the Coal Black Feather Company in Baltimore. He shipped a lot of them, too, don't you think he didn't.

My grandfather would get together with four or five other fellers and they'd travel from Cape Charles up the bay shooting canvasbacks and redheads. Then they'd ship them up to Baltimore for the big hotels. I don't believe there was even any laws against it then. Then the government come along and made these damn laws which made it even harder to make a living out here. What you've got to understand is that Smith and Tangier islands were settled around 1658 by people who came here to live on what they could get. There wasn't nothing here then and you either made it or you didn't, but the last damn thing you needed was some damn bunch of people who know nothing about it makin' laws to tell you what you can or can't do.

BEFORE outboard motors, we'd pole and shove our skiffs everywhere. One night, years ago in January, I set out with my skiff and big gun, south towards Horse Hammock Point. Well, I got to this gut, but couldn't get across it 'cause the tide was still too low, but just past that gut I could see about fifty geese sittin' out there feedin'. So I took my shotgun and crawled through the grass and down the beach to them and killed five. Then, back at the skiff I could get across the gut, but had to carry my punt gun across separately. Then I pushed down through the bay, almost to Tangier Island but still couldn't get to the other side of the bay across the bars. So I finally turned around and shoved back to Rhodes Point, all in one night. Today, you can't find anybody who'll push a skiff five feet.

I'd push all through those marshes settin' and emptyin' my traps, too. Set up to six at a time in water eight to ten inches deep, just the right depth for feedin'. You could do all right with them traps. I've seen fifty-nine pintails come out of one trap and that was good for around here. We didn't have to move them around much back then, 'cause it wasn't till after the thirties that the law started to show up regular out here.

Then, after they came, we couldn't get rid of them for nothin'. They'd show up in a big boat towing two or three smaller ones. They'd anchor, then split up, and go all through the marshes lookin' for traps. Bother the hell out of us. Christ, every time they see somebody out in a boat they'd think they were up to something illegal, but, hell, what can you do around here without one?!

My dad ran the store down at the wharf and I can remember hearing many stories down there about using the big guns [punt guns]. They'd push those skiffs all over the bay, from up the Holland Strait down to a place called the Knolls. Stay all night, most of the time and gun. You had to have just the right conditions to use one of the guns. Sometimes my grandfather would cover himself up with a blanket of seaweed, go to sleep, and wait for the tide to fall or the moon to raise up so he could shoot again. Now, you take the forepart of the night, the dark is coming out of the east so you have light still in the west. You'd push and paddle up from the east and have your light still in the west to see your flocks sittin'. Now, if you had the moon risin' in the east you try and get yourself right underneath it so the birds wouldn't see you comin'. Sometimes you could push that skiff over ten miles to get to a feedin' spot, then have to lie down in the boat, and use them hand paddles to get yourself all lined up.

You hear stories, especially from these damn anti-hunters, about how thousands of duck would be killed in one night, but I'm here to tell you it just wasn't true. You had to be as good with one of those punt guns as you was with a shotgun and sometimes better. 'Course, you could shoot a path right through them and twenty feet high but, if you didn't have just the right conditions, and set up right, you could miss real easy, too. Now, after you was within range, you'd shift your weight around to either lift up or drop the bow of the skiff, use the paddles to line up just right, and touch her off. You had to be real careful that she was chocked down good 'cause with one quarter of a pound of powder and a pound and a half of shot coming out of a one-hundred-pound gun, if she broke loose you could be in real trouble fast in that cold water. Now, if you was lucky enough to hit the flock, you go after your cripples first before they could head out to deep water and dive. 'Specially the canvasbacks and redheads, they'll dive like the devil.

189

HAVE you ever tasted swan meant? I'll tell you, the breast meat is just as good as a piece of roast beef, and it don't necessarily have to be a young bird either. I've shot them over three years old and they were just as good as a spring-hatched bird. Never tasted one that was strong, always mild. 'Course, very few ever get eaten. I think if they weren't so damn hard to pick, you'd see a lot more of them around on people's tables. 'Cause there's times you could go out there and kill a skiff load if you wanted to, but nobody does anymore, I guess.

When I was first gunnin' with my dad, about fifty years ago, we were down on Horse Hammock Point around Thanksgiving. I had my old double barrel loaded with what we called 3B shot, only about forty-six to a shell so it hit pretty hard. We set out our stool and waited and in come three bluebills, three sprigtails, and a swan. My dad says for me to take the swan, and he'd take the ducks. Now, as that old swan was sittin' there pickin' itself, I let him have it—didn't give him much of a chance with that shot. Yeah, we cooked him up for Thanksgiving, and I carried some of it over to this old feller that I hunted with sometimes who lived over in the woods.

One other time, a feller and me killed nine with two punt guns, each firin' ours off. One of them weighed over twenty-three pounds dressed. The last time I killed swans, I went down the bay one night, shot eight, picked and dressed them, and still only got a dollar a piece for them!

I USED to do quite a bit of gunnin' with Alan Smith who lives here in Tylerton. He worked up at South Marsh for a while at the club. That used to be one of the best gunnin' places in this area, over ten thousand acres of marsh, alive with ducks and geese. A damn good place for catchin' terrapin, too. I caught over two hundred one day up there, anyway.

They'd bait the hell out of the place. You could shoot canvasbacks just by stickin' your gun out the clubhouse window at times. Now, the state of Maryland got ahold of it, which is a lot better than havin' the federal government controlling it. The clubhouse is all but gone, but I'll bet there's still a lot of birds up there.

I remember one time I was out gunnin' with Alan and another fellow. They was up ahead of me and I'd already killed one bird when all of a sudden here comes the warden. He had an outboard and come right up on Alan. I was watching all this from where I was layin' so I figured I'd better hide my duck and gun, which I did. Then I headed back to my boat to wait. Well, damned if that warden didn't find the duck and gun, and here he comes again, up to my boat this time, ties up, and climbs right aboard.

"We've got reason to believe you're killin' birds illegally," he says, and, of course, with only one bird that he could find I wasn't.

But, he confiscated the gun and all twelve of the Ward brothers good decoys that I had on board, and off he went. So about a week later I got a notice in the mail to pay a thirty-dollar fine for illegal hunting, whatever the hell that meant since they never did catch me that day with the goods. Well, I paid it just so I could get my decoys and gun back. But that shows you what we was up against, even when we wasn't violating the law.

My brother and myself used to guide for Glenn L. Martin, the millionaire airplane builder from Baltimore who built the Martin Marauder during World War II. He was the original owner of Remington Farms up at Chestertown and at one time owned half the marsh you see here till he gave it all to the government. Except for that he was a good man.

He come down to the bay on his yacht and he'd gun for two or three days at a time. Used to keep a couple of houseboats moored out in the marsh together, all outfitted and ready to hunt and live out of. My brother and me would stay in one of them and him in the other and we'd take him gunnin' every day. Finally had to give it up 'cause of his health.

I remember this one time we'd been baitin' pretty heavy. Had about fifteen hundred pounds of corn out and this damn warden who'd been comin' around for a while came through our spot, dropped a dredge, and, of course, came up with corn. Now, we was watching all this happening so we got out of there fast. But later on, he caught up to the three of us and pesterin' us about whether we knew anything about the corn. What the hell did the damn fool think we were going to say? Yes?! Anyway, Mr. Martin was gettin' pretty mad by this time and asked him if he didn't have something more important to be doing rather than botherin' us about some damn corn. Next day Mr. Martin left for Baltimore and said he was gonna make some phone calls about that feller. I guess he did 'cause I never saw him again.

I WAS around doing it when you could use live geese and ducks, then they got tight on that and you couldn't do it no more. We raised our own geese and ducks then. Used to take our cripples and put them in with the tollin' birds till they got better, then we'd use 'em or let 'em go.

I've seen a brant and a goose with shot wings all crippled up, lie down on the marsh with those wings on the wet ground and stay there till the crippled wing rotted off. You wouldn't think they'd be that smart, but they are. See, as the wing's rottin' off, it's curing at the same time, so they don't bleed to death. Yes, sir, them tollin' birds could make all the difference in the world. You let them go and they'd swim out to a bunch of wild birds and swim them right back into your decoys. See, we'd pen them up at night and feed 'em good to keep them around. You could go out in the daytime and whistle and the whole flock would fly right to you. Now, if we was going to use them as live decoys in one spot, we put this band around their leg and attach a hook fastened to a line and anchor them down so they'd stick right there. You just couldn't beat them once they got calling.

193

Delbert "Cigar" Daisey

Photo: Dan Brown

DELBERT "CIGAR" DAISEY was born on Chincoteague Island, Virginia, on March 6, 1928. Raised by an aunt, he quickly took to life on the waters and marshes surrounding Chincoteague. Around 1940, he started carving miniature and working decoys for himself, being heavily influenced by the works of the great carvers Ira Hudson and Doug Jester. He quickly developed a style all his own and as early as the 1950s found a demand for his work. Among his clients were the DuPont family of Delaware.

His carving at first hardly brought in enough to support a family, and so Cigar took to doing what he knew best—fishing, catching turtles, crabbing, oystering, gunning, and duck trapping—to fill the void. One of the last surviving "outlaw gunners," Cigar had many close calls with both state and federal wardens, outsmarting some of the best of them for years until the one time when, "too tired," he was run down by a seaplane and caught.

Today, Cigar is recognized as one of the top carvers in the world. His birds, if you can buy them, bring large sums of money.

He still guns, but now "only within the bounds of the law" and can be found most days working on a bird or "holding court" in his carving shop behind his home with his many friends from the Island and all over the country.

He lives on Chincoteague Island with his wife and is the featured carver at the Chincoteague National Wildlife Refuge Museum.

Mᴇ and Clarence's brother trapped together one year. We caught sixteen hundred and twenty-one which wasn't a bad year, but it wasn't great either. If we got twenty-seven or twenty-eight hundred birds during trappin' season, we were doing all right. See, what you got to bear in mind is that you could've probably caught five times that many if you weren't all the time trying to buck the law. Sometimes they'd have twenty-some wardens out in the marshes trying to break you up. And if they didn't stop you trappin', they'd sure slow you up for a while. The best thing you could do was just sit tight till the sons of bitches left. So, in the meantime, you just bait spots heavy. I'd take ears of corn, five or six of them, and wire them together. Pile them, five or six feet tall sometimes, then I'd go out and stick them down with crab stakes in the mud. That way, it'd hold the corn down, and the ducks would stay in those spots. Then, when they left, I'd go back and set my traps. It was a big game, you know, and when you're young like that you enjoy the hell out of it. Sometimes we'd even try and stay right behind them when they'd go through the marshes. Or we'd leave traps out for them to destroy, just so they'd think they was really doing something. Yep, it was like a big checker game. They'd be tearin' up traps and we'd be right behind 'em settin' up new ones. We done what we pleased, back then.

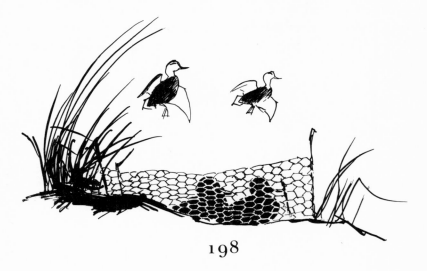

My neighbor over there started trappin' ducks right after he came home from World War II. We trapped side by side for two or three years then until he got his own rig together. He was a damn good trapper, too. Went to prison two times for it though. First time he got caught, Leon Cole caught him—him and Mark Daisey and Dallas Fish. They gave him six months at Petersburg, Virginia at the federal reformatory. The next year when he came back he went trappin' with me. We had a pretty good year. He got his rig together and the next few years he trapped by himself. Eventually, the "Peanut Man," Anthony Stephano, came to Chincoteague, looking for me, actually. Hell, he caught trappers and hunters all over the country.

Well, he was staying down at the hotel in town and 'course nobody knew who the hell he was; just another outsider. Well, my wife used to go down there and have a beer from time to time, and one day I guess he found out who she was and he asked her to find out if I had any ducks for sale. Hell, I had plenty of ducks then—live and frozen. Anyway, I told her to go back to the hotel and check his room. I wanted to know what kind of damn equipment he had there, if any, and if he didn't, maybe he was legitimate. So, she went back there and checked. When she came back, she told me there was no equipment, but he had a pair of those green lightweight gunning boots that I knew wardens wore so I told her just as sure as you were born that man's a damn game warden. You see, he told her he know'd me—met me—years ago, but I know'd I never did talk to him.

But, anyway, he got George the second time. George and Vern Lewis had a bunch of ducks over in Clarenfield Thornton's yard somewhere and he saw this Stephano over near there one day looking around. He told him, "You look like a damn game warden to me and if I know'd you was for sure I'd kill you."

'Course he was only kidding, just trying to scare off another outsider. Anyway, he caught him in an undercover setup
finally, and about a month later Bob Heinz and two or three
other federal agents caught him again in the act of settin' traps,
so they carried him to court and give him six months at
Allenwood, Pennsylvania for trappin'. When they let him out
six months later, the Fish and Wildlife wanted to send him to
court again for the undercover setup, but the judge threw it
out.

W H E N I was a little boy, I used to go with my father trapping ducks in a little thirteen-foot boat. Before outboard motors, we'd go out at night, empty the traps, and be back by daylight. Get a damn boatload sometimes. We've had so many that if the wind was blowing hard, we had to take them out of the boat and leave some of the bags till the next day so we wouldn't sink. We kept them alive as long as we could to keep them fresh. Then they could digest the corn, too. If they was full of corn, their damn throats stuck out to one side.

In those days, if they caught you trapping, they'd give you six months or five hundred dollars. Later they changed it to two years or two thousand dollars. Hell, a man can do six months standing on his head, but two years is a different story. My neighbor spent time for trappin' up at Allenwood, Pennsylvania. They call it the country club now, where they put all the crooked politicians. Anyway, he was with me the day they caught me with the airplane, but he got away in his boat. He'd just come back from Petersburg, a federal reformatory, and when we spotted the plane he said, "You know what they'll do to me if they catch me again, don't you?"

'Course, I did, so I told him to head for Black Point, hoping they'd come after me instead, and they did. Yep, he went to prison twice for trapping. He's not in real good health now, but I'll tell you, he was one hell of a man in his day. A great war hero, too.

HELL, I think it was 1966 Clarence caught fifty-five hundred black ducks. That's just about the best damn year I've ever heard of. One night I saw him and his wife coming home with someone else's rig, a boat loaded right up with bags of ducks. It wasn't uncommon for a trapper to go and take someone's rig to empty his traps. You just had to make sure you cleaned all the damn mud and feathers out of it when you'd bring it back so nobody'd know. In fact, there was one man down here who'd go down to his rig every morning to go crabbin'. He'd brag like hell about how good this engine he bought was. Christ, he'd always be telling you how it would start on the first pull. 'Course, he didn't know the damn thing was red hot from carryin' ducks in all night.

Another time, Clarence had somebody's rig out and broke the damn shear pin well. 'Course, he didn't have a spare with him or even a nail, so he shoved a gaff hook tip into it and broke it off. Then he limped back into the dock just before daylight. To this day I wonder what that guy thought when it went, and he saw the hook in there.

WE had this old abandoned place out in the marshes that we used as a watch house. It had a couple of pieces of furniture, a burlap bag hung for a door, and an old two-burner stove. We'd sit out there nights sometimes when we was working our traps, talk till all hours, and have us a little something to drink.

This one particular night around dusk, we'd already set all our traps and were sitting around the place when I spotted Jim Williams and another warden named Robinson from Cambridge coming into the creek in their little boat.

"Well," I said to the boys, "just as sure as we were born, those wardens been watching us."

Well, they weren't as sure as me about it, but I was, and I also knew I still had about sixty pounds of corn in my boat so I lit down to it, picked out the bag, carried it down the creek, and waded in with it up to my waist in water. Well, these wardens came right by me and didn't see me standing there. I still don't know how they didn't hear my heart beatin'. When they got a good way past me, I took off back to the house, and by now didn't have to convince the boys just who was in the marsh. Now, this one particular area that they was headed for was full of duck traps, so we followed behind them to see if they'd find any. When they got up to this gut, we could hear them cut their motor and by now it was dark so we poled up towards them, and George yelled out to them, "Hey, Captain, you out of gas?"

They yelled back that they were and shined this big old spotlight on us. When I saw this, I started my outboard up and eased out of there so fast my cigar lit up like a spotlight. Well, we got back to Chincoteague and went over to Jim Williams's house, hid in the honeysuckle patch and waited for him to come home, and when he did, we went back out and got our ducks.

204

I'D try and set my traps on Sunday nights figuring the law wouldn't be watching me. Plus it would give me more time to make a good set. Then, Monday morning I'd have plenty of ducks for my wholesale market. Come Thursday night I'd try and set again, but would do it Fridays regardless, to give me ducks for my local trade on weekends. I could've set every night, but I would've caught every damn one of them and you just can't be too greedy.

I remember one night in the early 1950s I'd been out emptyin' my traps, had about eight bags of black ducks, and my outboard broke down. I poled and paddled for a while until I got too tired. Then I gave it up for the night and lay down in the bottom of my boat to go to sleep. Now, it was pretty cold, but I was dressed right, and I had warm gloves and the bags of ducks to keep me warm. While I was sleeping, it snowed to beat hell, and when I woke up about nine o'clock, I was covered with snow, but still warm. Well, I could hear the boys coming out to look for me, and I figured they'd have some liquor with 'em to help get me going again. They did, but it was almost gone when they got to me. Well, I got myself back to the club, hid my ducks in a barn, and went in and had me some breakfast with the members who were surprised to see me come back alive. They thought I'd have frozen out there, and I might have if I hadn't had the bags of live ducks to keep me warm.

I HUNTED those marshes around Chincoteague daily. I'd hunt all over the bay, shoot diving ducks and puddlers, whatever the market wanted. If I knew that I had plenty of market for something, I'd go and get it.

I hunted when the weather was real bad and rough. That's when the market hunter was out, you know, when it wasn't fit for a man to be out.

We shot 'em over bait mostly, right down at dusk or late in the evening. Some places we'd call "daytime places"—that's where you'd go to hunt early in the morning and gun till about two in the afternoon. Then you'd go to your baited spot at night. That way you'd always kill the most. The most black ducks I ever shot was fifty-four in two hours over a baited spot, the second day of a freeze. When I say fifty-four, that doesn't count trash ducks: pintails, canvasbacks, gadwalls, and like that. Other than the pintails, there wasn't much of a market for the others. Anyway, I don't know how many I really killed that day, but it was a lot more than fifty-four.

You know, what really raised hell with the ducks was the outboard motor. Before that you could kill a lot of birds but it was hard to get out and back to your spots, especially if the wind was blowin' pretty good. Hell, with an outboard motor, I've left home at dark and gone twenty miles down to Palmer's Beach, killed geese as they fed under the moon, and by the crack of daylight I'd be up on the upper end of Cedar Island Beach laying next to a drinking hole shooting black ducks as they came in, then back to Chincoteague the next night.

I'd usually hunt by myself, but would take friends with me sometimes if they was hurtin' for money. "Stump jumpers," I'd call them if they didn't do it like me full time. We'd hunt over on the government land where we weren't supposed to, called it "huntin' on my uncle's property." We were a damn thorn in their sides, I'll tell you.

One time I ran into some of the boys over there just as I was getting ready to pick up and leave. Well, I put my bags of birds in my boat and left my decoys out for them to shoot over. They brought a hell of a lot of liquor with them and while they was gunning, I sat in the grass behind them and held onto it for them. Every time they'd kill a bird I'd give them a drink, and they killed about thirty-five or forty black ducks, so we had us a pretty damn good time.

SOMETIMES out in those marshes, I'd take some of those little Doug Jester decoys, split them open, and cook my food with them. That goes to show you how much decoys was worth back then. I never got any money for my decoys until about 1964. Until then, if somebody'd give you three dollars for one you'd be doing all right. But, hell, you could count on gettin' a dollar a piece for black ducks and that was pretty good money. Unless you raised broilers, it was about the only thing you could do to make a steady living, even then.

There was me and maybe two or three others who did it full time. You see, I was a damn fanatic over it, you know. I mean, I wanted to live in those marshes day and night and would have if I didn't have a family at the time. Anyway, I'd usually go out for two or three days at a time; leave home about 2 A.M. and head out to check my traps. Trappin' was real hard on the black duck, and, 'course, the tougher things got for me, the harder I'd be on them which ain't right, but that's the way that it was. I'm glad it's over now, for their sakes, but back then I would've killed the last one if I'd had the chance. Gunning, you could kill thirty or forty black duck a day if you were a good shot and had perfect conditions, but trappin' you could catch one hundred so easy it wasn't funny.

You'd bait an area for a couple of days till they were comin' in steady, then set your traps. They were funnel shaped from about four inches at the opening to about one foot at the top. Christ, those birds would push through to get to that corn like you wouldn't believe. Now, rather than trying to catch every damn one of them at once, what you'd do was trap yourself a reasonable amount and let some go back and tell the others about the food. This way you'd always have birds comin' in. Shit, I've seen 'em coming in as late as nine at night, solid rafts of them looking for the corn. 'Course, you had to be careful about the airplanes spotting the corn. It stands out like you wouldn't believe. Now, after trappin' one spot for a while, the birds would eat the marsh grass down to nothing, and you'd have a big bald spot that was easy to spot from the air so you'd have to keep moving your traps.

You know, people today, and especially the so-called conservationists, are real hard on duck trappers and market hunters but, hell, I've seen your so-called sportsman kill more than a market hunter would in one day, and he didn't have no use for the birds. In all the years I've worked around gunning clubs, the only real honest people that I gunned with were sportswriters, and I think they were just afraid of losing their jobs if they got caught—you know, if somebody talked.

I've lived the way the average millionaire sportsman would've liked to. February would come and I'd start my shad fishing. Eleventh day of April, I'd go for sturgeon and make caviar. One year I caught over eleven hundred of them. After shad, I go for sea trout [weakfish] till about the twenty-second of October. After that, they'd fade away. Then I always wanted to be trapping my first ducks by Halloween, so in the meantime I'd be baitin' just as many spots as I could. So, as soon as I put my fish nets away, I'd go right back to trappin' ducks. We'd always be hustlin'. Never had no trouble makin' a livin', but never made a hell of a lot of money either.

The bulk of the money I made back then was from trappin' ducks. Trappin' was much more effective than shooting 'cause you wouldn't scare the birds. You just had to worry about the wardens. Hell, they all knew your traps and who you were selling to. I used to sell to judges, doctors, members of the House of Delegates, all the damn professional people. I'd shoot mergansers, sometimes twenty-five to thirty a day from February to April, and sell them to the people who worked in the oyster shucking houses. The good birds, black ducks and pintails, I'd sell to the other people during the week. I'd sell one hundred at a time to some of the boys who'd ship them north. Then, on weekends, I had my local trade. I'd tie them up in pairs and wrap 'em in paper bags to sell to the local people. You know, somebody who just wanted a couple of ducks to eat. I never did ship any birds myself, but, like I said, I sold plenty to people who did. It just seemed the easy way to get caught.

In those days everybody hated the game warden. I know some of the boys would flip cigarette butts onto their car seats as they'd walk by, put water in their gas tanks, or even beat the hell out of them. They shot the hell out of one right next to me one day, gave him a load of sixes at thirty-five yards. It was in *Look* magazine sometime in 1945.

Mostly though, we'd just outfox them. I'd be going down the narrows to check my traps, see some man oystering that I'd know, and ask him if he'd seen "Big Red"—that's what we called them. If he'd seen somebody, he'd tell you when he was through, and what direction he was headed. Yep, you'd usually know when they was around. Sometimes they'd anchor a big old boat out in the bay, and three or four of them would come into the marshes and try to hide. On a real pretty day when I'd be out there, I'd get myself up a gut at lunchtime and lay right down in the bottom of my boat to rest. Then, if I heard a motor coming into the marsh, I'd take out my glasses and look them over.

There were lots of wardens around here then, and they could get pretty tough on a man at times. I was always afraid they was going to set me up, but they never did. I've had them close to me at times, damn close. Matter of fact, we had a warden here on Chincoteague named Jim Williams. He was a famous warden mentioned a lot in Walsh's *The Outlaw Gunner*.

Well, like I said, he lived right here. He was a big, heavy man, raised about eighteen children, and he destroyed more duck traps than any man alive, I believe. We'd watch him like *nothing*. I'd wait in a big honeysuckle patch next to his house till he came home, then go out and do whatever the hell I wanted to. He came to see me after he retired, just before he died, and told me how close he'd been to me sometimes. But, hell, I knew that. I've had them walk right by me when I'd be lying down, hiding in that marsh grass. I always figured that as long as I stayed in my area around Chincoteague I'd have the edge on them 'cause I know those marshes like you know your streets back home. You know, a red fox ain't real smart but he's wiry, scared, and always looking over his shoulder—if you live like that—and I tried to—you'll last a long time. If not, he'd get you surer than hell.

The only time they ever did get me was in the spring of 1952. Nine wardens chased me with an airplane and three boats. They never did catch me doing anything wrong, 'cause I got away from them—hid the decoys, gun, and bags of ducks. But when I walked back to the boat, they came up behind me and grabbed me by the shoulders. Damn near snatched my feet out from under me. They put me in a boat and took me to their dock where they put me in a car and carried me over to the bay side. They then landed the plane and took me to the courthouse in Accomack to a judge whose name I can't remember. He's dead now, I guess. Anyway, he talked to me

good as any man would. Matter of fact, he told me to go outside and sit on the courthouse steps till they had my trial. Finally, put a seventy-five-dollar fine on me and he cashed the check, and, I guess, kept the damn money. You see, the warden made the check out and had me sign my name to it. It was made out to the judge. I still got that check at home with his name on the back.

ME and Clarenfield Thornton used to hunt together around 1945. We had this old inboard boat about thirty-five feet long that we'd take down to Cedar Island and stay a week sometimes to hunt and trap ducks and muskrats, and catch oysters, clams, and terrapins. We'd put them all together and come home with what we'd call us a big trip, usually end up with a reasonable amount of money between us. You could sell the terrapins for anywhere from ten cents for a bull or heifer [small turtle] to one dollar for a good-sized one. Sometimes you'd get sixty or seventy different ones. Now, the way you'd catch them was to get yourself a stick, something like a broomstick, and walk down the edge of a gut right in the marsh. When you saw a little spot in the mud, sometimes about the size of a silver dollar and almost blue looking, you'd take that stick, put it in the hole, and lightly tap it up and down to see if there was something down there. If you felt the shell and heard kind of a hollow noise, you'd reach down and work your hand into that soft mud, grab ahold of him, and pull him out. They won't bite you no way then. Anyway, then you take him and wash the mud off him in the gut and put him in your burlap bag. You'd walk for miles doing that.

People don't do it much anymore, but Miles Hancock used to buy all ours back then. He was a big terrapin keeper and a great market hunter; never did hunt with him though. He passed on in his eighties, a right many years ago, and Homer Jones started to take over for him, but just about as soon as he got going good at it, he died too.

See, you had "keepin pens" where the tide would rise and fall through every day, and you couldn't feed them too much or they'd get fat and chafe themselves on their shells. They liked cut up minnows and crabs the best.

Now, during an election year around here you could sell all the terrapin you had. They'd use them at these big campaignin' dinners they have, to make terrapin soup. Yep, that was a big thing back then.

Hell, we didn't even have to bring no food with us. We'd eat what we trapped or shot, and at that time the beaches around here used to be covered in C-ration cans that they threw overboard during the war, I guess. You'd get yourself chocolate bars and even powdered eggs.

THERE just weren't that many people on Chincoteague back then who gunned for a living. Me and maybe two or three others, and they weren't at it full time like I was. I was a damn fanatic about it. I would have lived in those marshes day and night if I could've, but I had a family then so I come home from time to time.

I'd leave home way before daybreak, usually about two o'clock, and head out into the marshes to check my traps. Sometimes I'd stay out two or three days straight; just lie right down in my boat and sleep when I had to. Felt real good with that sun shining down on you, wake up with the stars shining bright on you. Damn near froze to death a couple of times. Woke up covered with snow. But, hell, I loved it, and it was the only way I knew of to support my family back then. I was making decoys, of course, but they weren't worth a damn at that time.

I would do some guiding down at the club, too, for extra cash. Bring my ducks in from the marsh and hide 'em at the club, then go get myself a party, take 'em out gunning for the morning or afternoon and pick up an extra twenty bucks. We was damn glad to get it, too. Hell, today the boys won't take you out for anything less than a hundred bucks. And what can you shoot but a few brant? Then you could shoot six per man and believe me you'd get six per man each time. The place was loaded with them. I even saw a white one once, but I didn't shoot it.

I shot an old Model 11 then, the type with the safety behind the trigger. Damn good gun, too. I just wore it out, that's all. Then, years back, a man gave me an 1100. That's the gun I still use today.

Never did use a dog of my own, though. I just never liked the idea of them getting into the boat and shaking themselves, wetting everything in sight. In fact, I do remember one time when I had a man and his dog with me from the club. The dog retrieved beautifully, but after every bird, he'd shake and soak us down. Then he'd be trying to get right up next to you to stay warm. Damn pain in the ass. But don't get me wrong, though. There's a lot of advantages to having a good dog. They just don't belong out in a marsh trapping. Hell, if the wardens start chasing you, you might have to leave him out there, and it just didn't seem fair.

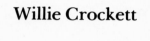

Willie Crockett

Born on Tangier Island in the Chesapeake Bay, February 3, 1939, Willie Crockett lived there until leaving to become a student at Columbia Bible College in South Carolina.

After graduating, he taught for a year, and then travelled for seven years throughout the United States as a practicing minister. Later, Willie settled on a commune on the West Coast, where he began to paint and write. Motivated by the intellectual environment there, he left the commune to resettle on Virginia's Eastern Shore, to devote himself full time to his painting. Today, with good reason, he is considered a collectible artist. His paintings, like his poetry, clearly reflect the landscape and way of life on the Eastern Shore, offering a rarely found insight into this unique way of life.

He lives with his family near his studio in Onancock, Virginia.

THERE's always been an intense rivalry between the Tangier and Smith islanders. Especially when it comes to crabbing and gunning. Those Smith Islanders are very tough people for the most part—meaner than rattlesnakes some of them. A section of Smith Island is legally part of Virginia, you

know, but to try and make one of them believe it is impossible. Smith Island is Smith Island to them, and they don't recognize no boundaries, especially ones set by the government.

Every year we'd go up there for a week or so gunning and live out of one of the gunning shacks. One morning we were all rigged out, and not too far away was a bunch of Smith Islanders rigged out too. Now, each time birds started coming into our rig, they'd shoot and scare the birds away. So, naturally we started doing the same damn thing to them. Each time birds started coming to their rig, we'd shoot. This went on pretty near an hour till the guy who was with me said, "You know, the wind is with us and I'm sure we could lay some shot right on 'em if we tried." So, he put a number two shell in his gun, pointed it up, and pulled the trigger. Sure enough, it worked. Shot rained all around their blind.

"That'll show 'em," Ed said, laughing.

Two minutes later we heard this "crack" and damned if a .30 shell didn't pass right through our blind.

"Got any more bright ideas, Ed?" I yelled as we fought with each other to get flat on the floor of that blind.

HERE'S a poem I wrote about the tourists on Tangier:

> If you get this mud between your toes,
>   You'll never go away.
> That's what they say.
>   So far we've all been lucky.
> The tourists all wear shoes,
>   And only spend the day.

THIS old boy Burt from Tangier was up gunning and trapping on Smith Island one time when a warden spotted him from a seaplane and started chasing him down. Burt ran through the marsh and back to his boat. Jumping in, he took off towards Tangier following the power lines that used to connect the two islands. Now, the warden was still chasing him with the plane but couldn't land 'cause Burt was in the only sheltered water protected by the high tension wires. Finally, he saw Burt pull up into this gut near a point and lie down next to his boat.

The plane flew over, and damned if the warden didn't shoot two holes right through the bottom of the boat. Now, old Burt was really stranded and to make matters worse, here come the plane landing right near him. Out jumped the wardens and Burt, with nowhere to go, sat down, and waited to take his medicine. They gave him a summons ticket, confiscated his gun and decoy rig, and flew him back to Tangier.

I saw myself in minnow ditches
On the surface of the tide looking down at someone
who was looking up at me.
I guess I'll always be there no matter what success or
failure fate may bring.
I'll be linked to those green waters, a sunburned face
and the salty beginnings of my youth.
I was so trusting to the ebbing tide
A forever child looking to see if my reflection would
predict some future on the flow.
Now I'm older but still reaching for myself, and the
broken image of my face keeps smiling through
the ebbing and the flood of the years.
Narcissistic child always laughing, yet never mocking
me.
We've always been together, always reaching for each
other—forever child.

WE had a fellow on Tangier Island named William Lankford. Old William was a good soul but he wasn't all there, if you know what I mean. He never did no gunning, of course, but you couldn't convince the warden of it for a while.

See, we had this unwritten rule on Tangier that after the season was legally closed and you'd go gunning, which, of course, everybody still did back then, that we'd always take our poorest rig of decoys and worst gun. This way if the law got lucky and caught you, we figured we wasn't really losing anything and we'd always give our name as William Lankford. That is, till they caught on sometime later.

After a couple of years of old William not showing up for his court appearances, they started to send out some lawmen to find him. They'd stop the first waterman they came across usually.

"Excuse me, I'm a sheriff from the mainland and we're looking for William Lankford. Do you know where we could find him?"

"William Lankford," they'd answer. "My God, has he been gunning again?"

'Course we never did let them find him.

Before I was old enough to make more than just a
    puzzle out of sex,
I spent my time shoving small boats up little ditches,
Catching green crabs, and trapping minnows in a jar,
Unaware that I was having so much fun.
In fact, the more I think about it, I tried to make it
    work instead of play.
But, somehow at the ending of each day, I dumped my
    crabs back in the ditch and let the minnows go.
And if I was having fun, I didn't want to know.